MAY 1997

j
B
CORTES, H.

WITHDRAWN

Hernando Cortes

These and other titles are included in The Importance Of biography series:

Alexander the Great
Muhammad Ali
Louis Armstrong
Clara Barton
Napoleon Bonaparte
Rachel Carson
Charlie Chaplin
Cesar Chavez
Winston Churchill
Cleopatra
Christopher Columbus
Hernando Cortes
Marie Curie
Amelia Earhart
Thomas Edison
Albert Einstein
Duke Ellington
Dian Fossey
Benjamin Franklin
Galileo Galilei
Martha Graham
Stephen Hawking
Jim Henson
Adolf Hitler
Harry Houdini
Thomas Jefferson
Chief Joseph
Malcolm X
Margaret Mead
Michelangelo
Wolfgang Amadeus Mozart
Sir Isaac Newton
Richard M. Nixon
Georgia O'Keeffe
Louis Pasteur
Pablo Picasso
Jackie Robinson
Anwar Sadat
Margaret Sanger
Oskar Schindler
John Steinbeck
Jim Thorpe
Mark Twain
Pancho Villa
H. G. Wells

Hernando Cortes

by
Stephen R. Lilley

Lucent Books, P.O. Box 289011, San Diego, CA 92198-9011

ALAMEDA FREE LIBRARY
2264 Santa Clara Avenue
Alameda, CA 94501

Library of Congress Cataloging-in-Publication Data

Lilley, Stephen R., 1950–
Hernando Cortes / by Stephen R. Lilley.
p. cm.—(The Importance of)
Includes bibliographical references and index.
ISBN 1-56006-066-2 (alk. pap.)
1. Cortés, Hernán, 1485–1547—Juvenile literature.
2. Mexico—History—Conquest, 1519–1540—Juvenile literature. 3. Conquerors—Mexico—Biography—Juvenile literature. 4. Governors—Mexico—Biography—Juvenile literature. [1. Cortés, Hernando, 1485–1547.
2. Explorers. 3. Mexico—History—Conquest, 1519–1540.]
I. Title. II. Series.
F1230.C835L56 1996
972'.02'092—dc20 95-1279
[B] CIP
AC

Copyright 1996 by Lucent Books, Inc., P.O. Box 289011, San Diego, California, 92198-9011

Printed in the U.S.A.

No part of this book may be reproduced or used in any other form or by any other means, electrical, mechanical, or otherwise, including, but not limited to, photocopy, recording, or any information storage and retrieval system, without prior written permission from the publisher.

Contents

Foreword

THE IMPORTANCE OF biography series deals with individuals who have made a unique contribution to history. The editors of the series have deliberately chosen to cast a wide net and include people from all fields of endeavor. Individuals from politics, music, art, literature, philosophy, science, sports, and religion are all represented. In addition, the editors did not restrict the series to individuals whose accomplishments have helped change the course of history. Of necessity, this criterion would have eliminated many whose contribution was great, though limited. Charles Darwin, for example, was responsible for radically altering the scientific view of the natural history of the world. His achievements continue to impact the study of science today. Others, such as Chief Joseph of the Nez Percé, played a pivotal role in the history of their own people. While Joseph's influence does not extend much beyond the Nez Percé, his nonviolent resistance to white expansion and his continuing role in protecting his tribe and his homeland remain an inspiration to all.

These biographies are more than factual chronicles. Each volume attempts to emphasize an individual's contributions both in his or her own time and for posterity. For example, the voyages of Christopher Columbus opened the way to European colonization of the New World. Unquestionably, his encounter with the New World brought monumental changes to both Europe and the Americas in his day. Today, however, the broader impact of Columbus's voyages is being critically scrutinized. *Christopher Columbus,* as well as every biography in The Importance Of series, includes and evaluates the most recent scholarship available on each subject.

Each author includes a wide variety of primary and secondary source quotations to document and substantiate his or her work. All quotes are footnoted to show readers exactly how and where biographers derive their information, as well as provide stepping stones to further research. These quotations enliven the text by giving readers eyewitness views of the life and times of each individual covered in The Importance Of series.

Finally, each volume is enhanced by photographs, bibliographies, chronologies, and comprehensive indexes. For both the casual reader and the student engaged in research, The Importance Of biographies will be a fascinating adventure into the lives of people who have helped shape humanity's past and present, and who will continue to shape its future.

Important Dates in the Life of Hernando Cortes

1485
Hernando Cortes is born in Estremadura, Spain.

1499
Begins study of law in Salamanca, Spain; fails to complete studies.

1504
Sails for Hispaniola. Farms an estate granted him by the island's governor, Nicolas de Ovando.

1511
Sails for Cuba with Diego Velasquez, who will become Cuba's governor. Helps conquer the island. Velasquez grants him an estate and later names him alcalde (mayor) of Santiago.

1518
Velasquez names Cortes to command expedition to Yucatan. Cortes spends his own fortune outfitting his forces.

1519
Lands in Yucatan. After defeating coastal Indians and Tlaxcalans, he recruits many Indians to his side against the Aztecs. Enters the Aztec capital, Tenochtitlan.

1520
Leads his men in the Noche Triste, the retreat from Tenochtitlan. Defeats an immense Aztec army at the Battle of Otumba.

1521
Having rebuilt his army and assembled a large force of Indian allies, Cortes captures and destroys Tenochtitlan. Begins to build Mexico City on the site of the ruined Aztec capital.

1524
Leads an expedition to Honduras to capture and punish Cristobal de Olid for exceeding his authority. His subordinates in Mexico (New Spain) revolt during his absence.

1526
Returns to Mexico physically weakened after grueling Honduran expedition. Indians greet him as beloved ruler. Faces investigation by colonial authorities for his actions during the conquest.

1528
Returns to Spain, asking King Charles I to name him governor of New Spain.

1529
King Charles declares Cortes captain-general of New Spain and marquess of the Valley of Oaxaca; these impressive titles are less than Cortes had expected.

1535
Commands an expedition that discovers the Gulf of California but finds no wealthy kingdoms comparable to those of the Aztecs or Incas.

1540
Hoping that King Charles will name him governor of New Spain and increase the size of his estate, Cortes again returns to Spain; joins Charles's ill-fated expedition to Algiers.

1547
Back in Spain but fallen from favor with Charles, Cortes plans to return to Mexico but dies near Seville, Spain.

A Sixteenth-Century Hero

By sixteenth-century standards, Hernando Cortes was a hero. In three years he conquered most of Mexico, the domain of the mighty Aztecs, an empire four times the size of his home country, Spain. His conquests added twenty-five million new subjects to the Spanish empire. He seized enough gold, silver, and gems to change the world economy. In turn, he made America appear as a land of myth and wonder that attracted adventurers to its shores for generations to come. He accomplished all this with fewer men than might attend a high school basketball game today.

For a time, the Aztecs and their neighbors believed that Cortes was Quetzalcoatl, the fair-skinned god, returning from the land where the sun rises to reclaim Mexico. The conquistador's secretary, Francisco Lopez de Gomara, considered him God's instrument, a combination missionary and warrior, the man who by persuasion and force converted the Mexican Indians to Christianity and put an end to their practice of large-scale human sacrifice.

Writing thirty years after the conquest of Mexico, Gomara praised Cortes's achievements:

Cortes receives a hero's welcome after winning a victory over the Aztecs. Today, many remember Cortes not as a hero but as a cruel tyrant and a destroyer of cultures.

> The Conquest of Mexico and the conversion of the peoples of New Spain . . . should be included among the histories of the world . . . because it was very great. . . . It was great . . . in the fact that many and powerful kingdoms were conquered with little bloodshed or harm to the inhabitants, and many millions were baptized who now

Thousands of Indians lost their lives during the brutal Spanish conquest. While many perished in battle, countless others died from diseases introduced to Mexico by the conquistadors, as a result of forced conversion, and also of slavery.

> live . . . as Christians . . . for they had been captives of the devil and would sacrifice and devour a thousand men in a single day.[1]

Death and Destruction

Certainly, Cortes's conquest did make Mexico a Christian nation, but not with small loss of life. Those who did not accept the Catholic faith voluntarily were converted by the sword, and thousands of Indians died in battle with the Spaniards. This policy of forced conversion made Bartolomé de Las Casas, missionary and champion of the people of the New World, Cortes's bitter enemy. Known as the Apostle of the Indies, Las Casas condemned Cortes as a cruel tyrant who brought about so many "slaughters, violences, injuries, butcheries, and beastly desolations" as to "strike a horror into future ages."[2]

Cortes and his conquistadors killed still more Indians in ways they had not intended and could not have anticipated. The Europeans carried smallpox, typhus, measles, and other diseases previously unknown to Mexico. These plagues, against which the Indians had no immunity, ravaged Mexico for generations afterward. Medical historian Frederick F. Cartwright estimated that of a total Mexican population of twenty-five million, over eighteen million died of diseases brought by the Spaniards.

The local inhabitants who did survive found themselves in a vastly changed land. Cortes destroyed the Aztec capital, Tenochtitlan, a city he considered the most beautiful on earth, and built Mexico City on its ruins. Forced into slavery by the Spaniards, the people of Mexico provided the labor that reshaped the land according to the conquerors' vision. Their hands pulled down the ancient cities and rebuilt them on European patterns. Their labor cultivated the lands granted to their European masters by the king of Spain. Their work helped erase their own cultural heritage, a heritage as ancient as any on earth.

As European standards changed their environment and culture, the native peoples changed. The native population intermarried with the Spanish conquerors to produce mestizos, people of mixed Spanish and Indian heritage. During the conquest, the daughter of an Indian noble bore Cortes's son Martin. Thus the conquerors were altered by the conquered. Racially Mexico became a blend of the Old World and the New.

The Impact on Spain

The conquest also changed Spain forever. Although his motives for conquest included personal greed, Cortes also saw himself as a servant of the Spanish monarchs: Ferdinand II, who died in 1516, and then his grandson, who ruled Spain as Charles I. Accordingly, Cortes wished to make Spain more powerful through his conquests, and in this he succeeded. For a time Spain ruled the greatest empire on earth. The Spaniards used the resources of the New World to enrich the Old. By 1519 Spain already held some Caribbean islands that produced some gold, but nothing like the vast amounts Cortes's conquests yielded. The huge quantities of gold seized from the Aztecs spawned legends of golden cities throughout the Americas. In part inspired by Cortes's example, Francisco Pizarro conquered the rich Inca empire in South America, putting still more gold at Spain's disposal.

For decades after Cortes's conquests, ships carried gold, silver, and precious gems across the Atlantic Ocean to Spain. Spanish monarchs used the wealth to build the most powerful military machine in western Europe. Ironically, the wealth Cortes and his king used to enrich Spain

Cortes's conquest of Mexico and the riches it brought to Spain inspired other Spaniards to conquer the rich Inca empire in South America. This illustration depicts Cortes's successors beating the enslaved South American natives.

A Magnificent Culture

Cortes marveled at the magnificence of Aztec culture when he first encountered it. Writing of archaeology in Gods, Graves, and Scholars: The Story of Archaeology, *C. W. Ceram suggests why Cortes destroyed a way of life that fascinated him.*

"Cortes was a conqueror. . . . Beauty was of interest to him only when it was exchangeable for gold, and greatness only as something against which to measure his own. He was concerned with profit for himself and his Hispanic Majesty [Charles I], and at most with furthering the supremacy of the Cross [the Catholic Church], but certainly not the advancement of knowledge. . . . Barely a year after he had met [the Aztec emperor] Moctezuma [Montezuma] for the first time, Moctezuma was dead. In less than another year, the splendor of Mexico was destroyed. . . .

Cortes's reaction to Aztec culture is astonishing. Like the majority of contemporary eyewitnesses, he completely ignored the might and meaning of the people whom he brought under the Spanish heel. . . . The thought apparently never entered his head that rather than destroying a barbaric kingdom of savages, he had 'beheaded a culture as the passerby sweeps off the head of a sunflower.'"

ultimately helped bankrupt it. Overspending on the military, coupled with inflation caused by a sudden influx of gold, ruined the Spanish economy by the end of the sixteenth century.

From a sixteenth-century point of view, Cortes achieved greatness because of his conquests. However, the world of the 1990s condemns conquerors. Modern social scientists emphasize the right of a people to choose their own way of life, as well as the value of ethnic diversity and the importance of preserving each distinct culture. In contrast, Cortes deliberately destroyed the Aztec culture. Living by the dictates and expectations of his own day, Cortes did not fully consider the consequences of the changes he made in the world he had invaded, nor did he question his right to make those changes. Neither his times nor the land of his birth encouraged him to ponder the issue.

Chapter 1 The Call of Adventure

The high plains of Spain are called Estremadura. Here castle fortresses stand atop hills that once marked the frontier of the *reconquista* (the wars to reconquer Spain from the Moslems). Once Spanish warriors in the name of Christ had forced Arab Moslems from this land in a struggle lasting into the fifteenth century. A home to herdsmen, the land also nurtured warriors. The men of Estremadura were, in the words of historian Hammond Innes, "adventurers, soldiers of fortune, men born to lead in an age of medieval chivalry when the only proper activity for a gentleman was to fight."[3]

Born in Estremadura in 1485, Hernando Cortes grew to manhood among soldiers who had conquered Spain for their king and their Catholic faith. In those days, to be Spanish was to be Catholic, and young Hernando developed an uncompromising devotion to the church and a determination to convert the infidels, or nonbelievers. His father, Martin Cortes de Monroy, had served Spain honorably as a captain of infantry, but he and his wife, Catalina, did not plan for Hernando to become a soldier. As people of modest income, Martin and Catalina Cortes felt their son could be inexpensively trained for an honorable career as an attorney. When Hernando reached age fourteen, he went to Salamanca to study law but soon became bored with school. Much to his parents' dismay, in 1501 he returned home without completing his law degree. His time had not been wasted, however. In law school Hernando developed considerable skill as a writer. Occasionally, he composed poetry. More importantly, he gained an understanding of Spanish law that later served him well.

Instead of a quiet life as a lawyer, the young Cortes longed for the adventures Spain's global conquests offered. A young man with a strong sword arm could fight

Spanish conquistadors land in the Americas. Their tales of adventure and vast riches piqued the interest of the young, restless Cortes.

in Spain's European wars or in the conquest of the Americas. In those days, the Atlantic seaports buzzed with tales of the Americas, their vastness, and their wealth—and of limitless opportunities for adventure. Sensing that his destiny lay beyond the setting sun, Hernando arranged to sail with Nicolas de Ovando to the West Indies, as the Spanish then called their Caribbean islands. An Estremaduran and a friend of the Cortes family, Ovando had been appointed governor of the island of Hispaniola [present-day Haiti (west) and the Dominican Republic (east)]. While Ovando prepared to sail, Cortes decided to pay one more visit to a young married woman with whom he had become romantically involved. He climbed a garden wall under cover of darkness to avoid detection by the woman's husband.

As he quietly walked along the top of the wall approaching his ladylove's apartment, some badly cemented stones came

The Lure of Gold

The conquistadors risked their lives in the most dangerous undertakings of their times. In this excerpt from Europe in Transition: 1300–1520, *historian Wallace K. Ferguson writes of the Spanish explorers' motives and character.*

"It was not only the dwindling hope of reaching India . . . that drove countless adventurers to their death . . . in the steaming jungles of Central America. The lure of gold was . . . [a] powerful . . . incentive although no great quantity was found until, in 1519, Hernando Cortes fought his way to the uplands of Mexico and launched the conquest of the Aztec kingdom of Montezuma. The first stages of discovery, conquest and colonization were largely the work of independent adventurers, the greedy, savage and indomitable conquistadores who fought the Indians, the climate and one another to find wealth that few of them lived long to enjoy."

Christopher Columbus returned to Spain with exciting stories of gold and riches in the New World. Lured by the prospect of easy wealth, Cortes booked passage on a voyage to Hispaniola.

loose and the wall collapsed, sending Cortes crashing to the ground. Aroused by the noise, the woman's husband ran to the garden. There he found his wife's lover lying dazed among the rubble. Enraged, the jealous husband swore to kill Cortes on the spot. Fortunately for Cortes, the young lady's elderly mother persuaded her son-in-law to spare the injured intruder.

Cortes's injuries healed slowly, and he contracted a fever that came and went, leaving the youth unable to accompany Ovando's fleet when it sailed for the West Indies. The opportunity for adventure had passed.

Restless as always, Cortes wandered aimlessly throughout Spain for most of 1504. In November of that year, Christopher Columbus returned to Spain from the last of his voyages, telling tales of gold in the New World. Hearing the stories and dreaming of easy wealth, Cortes returned home and asked his parents to finance his passage to Hispaniola. By now convinced that their son would not take up a quietly respectable life, Martin and Catalina Cortes gave Hernando the money for a trip to the Indies.

Cortes in Hispaniola

In 1504 Hernando Cortes booked passage aboard a ship carrying trade goods to the Indies. Alonso Quintero, the captain with whom Cortes sailed, was to make the voyage in the company of four other ships from Spain. At the first stop, the Canary Islands, off the coast of Africa, the ships were reprovisioned for the next leg of the journey. Quintero, who saw the other captains as competitors, slipped away one night, hoping to arrive in Hispaniola ahead of the others so he could sell his cargo first.

A Devout Catholic

Cortes grew up in a devout Catholic family. In his biography, Cortes: The Life of the Conqueror, *Francisco Lopez de Gomara offers some insights into Cortes's devotion to Christianity.*

"As an infant Hernando Cortes was so frail that many times he was on the point of dying; but by an act of devotion made on his behalf by his wet nurse, Maria de Esteban . . . he recovered. What she did was to make a lottery of the names of the Twelve Apostles and give him as advocate the last name to be drawn, which turned out to be that of St. Peter, to whom she offered several masses and prayers, with which it pleased God that he should be cured. So he took St. Peter . . . as his special advocate, and became so strongly attached to him that every year he celebrated his feast day. . . . He was devout and given to praying; he knew many prayers and psalms by heart. . . . He ordinarily gave a thousand ducats [coins] a year to charity, and sometimes lent money for alms, saying that with the interest he would expiate [make amends for] his sins."

Not long after Quintero's departure, a violent storm tore the masts from his vessel, and the crippled ship limped back to the Canaries. Remarkably, the other captains agreed to wait for Quintero to complete his repairs, and all five vessels sailed for the Indies together. Again Quintero tried to elude his competitors. Seizing the first favorable wind, he sailed away from the rest. Enjoying a comfortable lead, Quintero soon became hopelessly lost. He blamed his pilot, his pilot blamed him, and the crew and passengers, some of whom feared they would land on a Caribbean island inhabited by cannibals, found renewed interest in the power of prayer.

Days passed without sight of land or other ships. Supplies ran short, and the thirsty travelers survived by collecting rainwater. Cortes's adventure seemed about to end with his death at sea. At last, a white dove landed on the ship's yardarm. The passengers and crew rejoiced at the land bird's miraculous appearance. Overjoyed, Quintero noted the direction the dove flew when it left the ship and set course in the same direction. Four days later, Quintero's ship reached Hispaniola and found that the others had already arrived and sold their goods.

Safely ashore, Cortes reported to the office of the governor. Although Ovando had left, his secretary advised Cortes to apply for a grant of land and workers. The Spanish government tried to make the settlements in the New World self-sustaining by giving estates to colonists and assigning native laborers to cultivate the soil and work the mines. Called the *repartimiento* system, the policy continued under one name or another, with some modifications, for decades.

The young adventurer made it clear that he had no interest in farming but wanted instead to grow rich quickly in gold prospecting. "Cortes, whose notion was that he had only to arrive in order to be weighted down with gold," wrote Gomara, "scorned the advice, saying he preferred mining."[4] Ovando's secretary warned the impetuous nineteen-year-old that growing rich from mining required hard labor and good luck.

By the time the governor returned, Cortes had decided to heed the secretary's advice. Ovando gave his young friend a land grant and appointed him notary of the town council of Azua. Cortes raised hogs on his estate and profitably sold salt pork to ships leaving the island. He also joined Ovando's lieutenant, Diego Velasquez, on military expeditions to put down native rebellions, but historians know few of the details.

However, the reasons for the native revolts were clear. The Indians were protesting the repartimiento system by which Spanish settlers relocated, abused, and enslaved the Indians. At first the Indians offered little resistance, but in time they escaped to the hills and fought Spanish attempts to reenslave them.

Describing Spanish attacks on the Indians, Bartolomé de Las Casas, a Spanish

Hispaniola natives subjected to the repartimiento *system of relocation, abuse, and enslavement revolt against their Spanish oppressors.*

priest who fought for Indian rights in the sixteenth century, wrote that the Indians

> fled from them to the mountains, therefore they hunted them with their hounds, whom they bred up and taught to pull down and tear the Indians like beasts. . . . Those whom their pity did think fit to spare, they would send away with their hands half cut off, and so hanging by the skin.[5]

Las Casas's accounts are truly grisly, but they may at times represent the writer's imagination rather than his experience. Intent on portraying the conquering Spaniards as villains, the priest often relied on graphic hearsay.

Cortes in Cuba

As the Spanish brought Hispaniola under their control, lands farther west beckoned to Cortes. In 1508 he considered sailing with Diego de Nicuesa, who had received a grant from Ovando to conquer and colonize what is now Honduras. Cortes fell ill and remained behind, but the illness proved a blessing, for disaster struck Nicuesa's expedition. Disease, shipwreck, and defeat in battle plagued the fleet at every turn, and Nicuesa went down with his ship in the Gulf of Mexico. Saved yet again from a watery death, Cortes found other opportunities. When in 1511 Velasquez took a military force to conquer

As Quick as Lightning

Cortes's manner and appearance helped him command respect. Drawing on accounts written by Cortes's followers, Paul Horgan describes him in Conquistadors in North American History.

"His bearing was lordly yet genial. He used his charm both as a gift to bestow and a weapon to wield. He could endure all which his soldiers endured and more. His mind was quick as lightning, but his more important thoughts were never known unless he meant them to be. . . . His imagination was powerful, and he was equal to it in his acts. Even under difficulty, if he wanted a thing to come true, he seemed able to compel it to do so. If most men were governed by events, it seemed the other way round with him. His face was pale and his expression usually serious, though he could be wonderfully cheerful, especially in adversity. . . . He was black-haired and he wore his beard thin. Those of a great horseman, his legs were somewhat bowed. In anger the veins of his throat swelled visibly, and in great anger he would refuse to speak."

Cuba, Cortes went along as his countryman's clerk and treasurer.

Cortes developed valuable administrative skills on the Cuban expedition. As Spain's armies conquered territory, they seized spoils of war including gold, jewels, and slaves. The expedition's commanders, officers, and common soldiers each received a share. Spain's king always claimed 20 percent of the loot, the "king's fifth." As clerk and treasurer, Cortes tallied the amounts of booty and made sure the king received his share. He also remained in the eye of Velasquez himself, who later launched the conquest of Mexico. The older Spaniard admired Cortes's courage and ability, and common soldiers found themselves drawn to his cheerfulness and ready wit. The Cuban conquest groomed Cortes for the larger tasks that lay ahead.

As Cuba's governor, Velasquez divided the land and Indian labor force among the Spanish soldiers and settlers, and Cortes received a generous allotment. Under Velasquez, the Spaniards enslaved the native people of Cuba much as they had done to the inhabitants of Hispaniola. The Indian populations were virtually exterminated. Cortes considered the Spanish colonization of Cuba wasteful and destructive. When he later commanded his own expedition, he tried to avoid repeating Spain's mistakes in Cuba.

Cortes developed his Cuban estate into a profitable enterprise. Settling at the new town of Santiago de Baracoa, he imported cattle from Europe to start his herd and put the Indians living on the land to work mining gold. This labor arrangement was one of the benefits to settlers offered by the *encomienda* system, which was intended to be an improvement over the repartimiento. According to the terms of the encomienda, Cortes was required to protect the Indians under his control and to teach them the Catholic faith. Furthermore, Indians were not to be enslaved, and limits were placed on the demands a settler could make on their labor. Despite the good intentions of the system's architects, the encomienda differed little from the repartimiento. The Indians were still enslaved and often were worked to death.

Indian women of a conquered territory are captured and forced into slavery by Spanish conquistadors.

Cortes Quarrels with Velasquez

In Cuba, Cortes found a distraction more powerful than gold—the beautiful Spanish-born Catalina Xuarez. Catalina's brother had brought his family to Cuba hoping to find rich husbands for his sisters. With men making fortunes quickly and women scarce in Cuba, the Xuarez sisters' prospects seemed good. According to Gomara, Cortes courted and promised to marry Catalina but later attempted to back out of the arrangement. Meanwhile Velasquez had fallen in love with another of the sisters and, hearing that Cortes had rejected Catalina, ordered him arrested and put in the stocks for reasons that remain unclear.

Thus Cortes, having become Velasquez's enemy both personally and politically, joined a group of settlers who disliked the governor and plotted to work for his downfall. According to the plan, Cortes was to sail to Hispaniola in a small boat and complain to the colonial authorities. Velasquez discovered the plot, however, arrested Cortes, and placed him once more in the stocks. The governor might even have ordered Cortes hanged, but influential citizens persuaded him to be merciful.

Cortes, fearing that the governor would deny him a fair trial, picked the locks (or bribed a guard to release him), overpowered a guard, took the guard's sword and shield, and lowered himself from a window to the street below. Then he fled to a nearby church for sanctuary. According to ancient tradition, a fugitive receiving sanctuary could not be arrested as long as he remained in the church that had taken him in, and the governor did not want to use force in a holy place. Velasquez posted guards outside the church, however, to arrest Cortes if he attempted to leave.

Impatient after a few days of sanctuary, Cortes stepped outside the church walls.

Cortes was arrested for plotting the downfall of his enemy, Cuban governor Diego Velasquez (pictured). The governor later forgave Cortes, and even chose him to lead an expedition to the Yucatan.

Immediately, one of Velasquez's men, Juan Escudero, grabbed him from behind and pinned his arms. Within seconds, several more of the governor's men seized Cortes, leaving him helpless. Cortes soon found himself aboard a ship that would take him to Hispaniola for trial. This time Velasquez shackled Cortes by his ankles, but one night before the ship was to sail, Cortes, after hours of struggle, managed to pull his ankles free. In the darkness, he crept across the deck, dropped over the side of the ship into a small boat, and rowed toward land. As he neared the shore, the water surged and swirled, nearly capsizing the boat. A strong swimmer, Cortes plunged into the water, fought his way through the waves to land, and again took refuge in the church.

Upon learning what had happened, the governor, weary of the long standoffs, sent word to Cortes that if he came out peacefully, he would be met once more in friendship. The fugitive left the church, made peace with Velasquez, and later married Catalina. Cortes could not have restored his relationship with the governor at a better time, for Velasquez and his impetuous young friend were soon to need each other. Once again, unknown lands to the west called to Cortes.

Yucatan Is Discovered

Velasquez had already sent one of his lieutenants, Francisco Hernandez de Cordova, to search for those unknown lands. In 1517 Cordova discovered the Yucatan peninsula on what is now the eastern edge of Mexico. After many battles, he returned to Cuba. Before he died of wounds suffered at the hands of the Indians, however, he told of a warlike people who lived in a new land rich in gold and silver.

Velasquez wanted to be the first of Spain's colonial governors to claim mainland territory and its wealth, but Spanish law left doubts as to who had the legal right to settle the new lands. The law required would-be governors of regions not yet under Spain's dominion to obtain permission from Spain itself or from the colonial government of Hispaniola. The first governor to establish a colony might make a stronger claim to rule the land. Velasquez wanted to be that governor.

Cortes's Ideas on Colonization

Sixteenth-century conquerors often sought only quick plunder. In his introduction to Hernan Cortes: Letters from Mexico, *historian J. H. Elliott says that Cortes's experiences in Hispaniola and Cuba taught him the need to develop Spain's colonies for long-term returns.*

"[Cortes] was the only one among the conquistadors who was able to grasp the fact that the wealth of America depended on the planned exploitation of all her resources. Cortes had seen for himself the ruin of the Antilles [Cuba and Hispaniola] by the dissipation of the land and its inhabitants in the rush for quick returns, and he was not prepared to watch this dismal example repeated in Mexico. His writings are full of requests that he should be given assistance to develop Mexican agriculture and adapt it to European requirements by introducing crops and the breeding of sheep and cattle that had proved so successful in . . . areas of Spain. . . . Although he was as greedy for booty as any of his foot soldiers [he wanted the long-term political power and] personal wealth offered by the governorship of a prosperous colony."

He tried both approaches. First, he began the long legal process of obtaining permission to establish a colony. In the meantime, in 1518, he sent his nephew, Juan de Grijalva, to explore the region. Velasquez seemingly wanted Grijalva to go beyond his orders and set up a colony in Yucatan, although the governor did not say this specifically. By avoiding a clear-cut order, Velasquez had technically obeyed the law but still might claim the right to rule the region.

For eight months, Grijalva explored the Yucatan coast and the surrounding islands. Some Indians welcomed the Spaniards and traded cotton cloth, fine featherwork, and objects of gold and silver for inexpensive Spanish goods such as shirts, beads, and mirrors. In all, Grijalva's expedition brought back twenty thousand pesos' worth of Indian goods, a handsome return on their investment. The Spanish expedition paid a higher price in human lives—thirty soldiers died in battles with the Mayans, who ambushed Grijalva's men as they came ashore to reprovision. Although the troops, dazzled by the land's wealth, begged Grijalva to plant a colony despite the risks, the governor's nephew insisted that his orders gave him no specific authority to settle the land. Had Grijalva been more daring and resourceful, he might have led his forces inland and triumphantly returned with Aztec gold. Instead he sailed for Cuba and missed his chance to be remembered for all time as the conqueror of Mexico.

News of Grijalva's treasure raced throughout Cuba. Men had grown wealthy in a few years mining Cuban gold. Now Yucatan promised even greater riches.

Juan de Grijalva was sent by his uncle, Governor Velasquez, to explore the Yucatan peninsula. He returned with expensive goods, but his timidity prevented him from conquering the Indians and establishing a colony there.

When he heard that Grijalva had not planted a colony, Velasquez became so angry that he refused to see his kinsman at all. Time was running out. The governor needed a new man to lead an expedition: Someone he could trust not only to seize Yucatan but to hand over the lion's share of the riches. Someone bold enough to go beyond his written instructions and establish a colony. Someone with enough personal wealth to pay most of the costs of outfitting a force to subdue the warriors of Yucatan. Someone willing to risk everything for God, glory, and gold.

Chapter

2 The Captain-General

Many Spanish adventurers would happily have returned to Yucatan under Juan de Grijalva's command, but Grijalva's timidity had already displeased Velasquez. The impetuous Cortes provided the governor a practical alternative. The two had settled their earlier disputes, and Velasquez had sponsored Cortes's marriage to Catalina Xuarez. More importantly, Cortes's performance in the Indian rebellions had impressed the governor.

The commander of the Yucatan expedition would need military experience and sufficient wealth to pay at least part of the expenses. Cortes had amassed a considerable fortune through mining and farming since his arrival in Cuba. Taking advantage of his financial success, the young Estremaduran lived lavishly, entertaining guests on a grand scale and outfitting his wife in costly wardrobes. Now he had other uses for his money.

Cortes knew that Velasquez was searching for someone to command the Yucatan expedition and quietly campaigned for the job. He made a secret pact with the governor's secretary, Andres de Duero, and the king's accountant, Amador de Lares. Lares and Duero agreed to persuade Velasquez to appoint Cortes captain-general (military commander) of the expedition in exchange for a share of any profits that resulted. The deal struck, Lares and Duero constantly reminded Velasquez of Cortes's leadership abilities. They also emphasized his willingness to obey orders, an important consideration in an age of slow communications. Velasquez followed their advice and named Cortes captain-general of the expedition, much to the dismay of several of the governor's relatives who also wanted the position.

Cortes's skill and bravery in dealing with Indian revolts influenced Governor Velasquez's decision to appoint him captain-general of the Yucatan expedition.

Cortes Sails for Mexico

One Sunday morning soon after the appointment of the captain-general had become known, Cortes and Duero accompanied Velasquez as he walked to mass. A buffoon known to the Spaniards as "the mad Cervantes" scurried alongside Velasquez taunting and warning him that Cortes was not to be trusted. "What a captain you have chosen, Don Diego," he shouted. "Take care, Don Diego, or he may run off with your fleet, for he knows how to look after himself, as everybody can tell you!"[6] Duero, realizing that some of Velasquez's relatives had hired the clown to undermine Cortes, slapped him and ordered him to hold his tongue.

Velasquez soon found reason to believe the buffoon's predictions. The new captain-general took on regal trappings, adding a plume to his hat and donning a velvet cloak trimmed with gold. He also wore a gold chain with a medallion signifying that he held the office of *alcalde* (mayor) of Santiago. Cortes sent out a proclamation promising all who joined him gold, silver, and encomiendas in the new land. From all over Cuba, adventurers flocked to his banner. More than 350 fortune seekers joined him at Santiago.

Cortes's growing army and increasing popularity worried Velasquez. The governor's relatives warned him that the new captain-general would prove uncontrollable; they knew that Cortes had invested all his money and mortgaged his estate to equip the fleet while Velasquez had risked little of his own wealth. Once he sailed, Cortes would be anxious to recover his investment and might ignore the governor's orders and neglect his financial interests. At one point, Velasquez tried to persuade Cortes to resign his command and promised to repay the money he had al-

A Great and Beautiful Enterprise

Both Cortes's friends and his enemies admired his persuasive abilities. In Cortes: The Life of the Conqueror, *Francisco Lopez de Gomara reconstructs Cortes's speech to his men on departing from Cuba.*

"I am embarking upon a great and beautiful enterprise, which will be famous in times to come. . . . I know in my heart that we shall take vast and wealthy lands, peoples such as have never before been seen, and kingdoms greater than those of our monarchs.

We are engaging in a just and good war which will bring us all fame. Almighty God, in whose name and faith it will be waged, will give us victory. . . .

If you do not abandon me, . . . I shall not abandon you, I shall make you in a very short time the richest of all men who have crossed the seas. . . .

Go your way now content and happy."

ready invested. Well aware of the governor's misgivings, Cortes politely refused and reassured him that the expedition would make them both rich.

Cortes decided to sail quickly before Velasquez revoked his authority. In November 1518, he sailed from Santiago for the town of Trinidad, collecting men and provisions as he traveled. In the meantime, having learned that Cortes had bribed Lares and Duero, Velasquez sent letters to his brother-in-law, Francisco Verdugo, the mayor of Trinidad, ordering the fleet detained and Cortes arrested. When confronted, the silver-tongued Cortes assured Verdugo that he was loyal to Velasquez and persuaded him not to carry out the order. Verdugo, fearing that Cortes's men would revolt if their leader were arrested, left the captain-general unmolested in Trinidad for ten days. Cortes even collected provisions from one of Velasquez's estates without interference.

The governor's temper flared when he learned that Cortes had slipped through his fingers. Bernal Diaz del Castillo, a soldier in Cortes's army who later wrote a detailed account of his leader's exploits, described Velasquez's reaction:

> The Governor roared with rage. . . . He swore Cortes was mutinous . . . [and sent orders to his relatives and subordinates] urgently begging them [not] to let the fleet sail, and to arrest Cortes immediately and send him to Santiago de Cuba under a strong guard. . . . Everyone took Cortes' part . . . while as for us soldiers, we would have given our lives for the Captain.[7]

Even though his fleet was not fully provisioned, Cortes decided to leave Cuba before Velasquez stopped him. According

Bound for Mexico, Cortes's fleet sails out of the Santiago harbor. Cortes lured many men to his army with promises of fame, glory, and enormous wealth.

to historian William Prescott, the captain-general inspired his men with a speech before the expedition departed:

> He told them they were about to enter on a noble enterprise, one that would make their name famous to after ages. He was leading them to countries more vast than any yet visited by Europeans. "I hold out to you a glorious prize," continued [Cortes], "but it is to be won by incessant toil. . . . If I have laboured hard and staked my all on this undertaking, it is for the love of that renown, which is the noblest recompense [payment] of man. . . . You are few in number . . . but . . . the Almighty, who has never deserted a Spaniard in his contest with the infidel, will shield you. . . ."
>
> The rough eloquence of the [captain-] general . . . sent a thrill through the bosoms of his martial audience; and . . . they seemed eager to press

forward under a chief who was to lead them . . . to battle [and] triumph.[8]

On February 18, 1519, the tiny fleet sailed from the westernmost tip of Cuba for the island of Cozumel off the coast of Yucatan. The force hardly appeared adequate for the conquest of a great empire, but the captain-general expected to encounter only scattered tribes, as in Hispaniola and Cuba. In all, Cortes commanded 11 ships, 32 crossbowmen, 13 musketeers, 508 foot soldiers, and 100 sailors. Their equipment included 14 cannon of varying sizes and 16 horses.

As the little force got under way, Cortes ordered his banner, a white flag bearing blue flames and a cross, unfurled. Inscribed along its edge in Latin were the words "Friends, let us follow the Cross, and with faith in this symbol we shall conquer."[9]

Ambitious young officer Pedro de Alvarado, a veteran of the Grijalva expedition, joined Cortes on his journey to the New World.

Cortes in Cozumel

The elements tested the conquistadors' faith almost immediately. A storm scattered the fleet, and Cortes arrived at Cozumel two days after the ships commanded by one of his young officers, Pedro de Alvarado. Upon seeing the Spanish ships, most of the Indians abandoned their town (also called Cozumel) and hid. Alvarado, a veteran of the Grijalva expedition, was anxious to find gold; he looted the town and captured three Indians.

When Cortes saw what Alvarado had done, he ordered the Indians' possessions returned to them immediately. Although he was capable of cruelty, Cortes realized that his expedition would enjoy more success if the Spaniards gained the natives' confidence and used force sparingly and purposefully. Cortes gave the Indians a few trade goods as gifts. Through an Indian interpreter named Melchior, who had been captured in Yucatan during Grijalva's expedition, Cortes called the island's town chiefs to meet him.

The next day, the chiefs and the town's inhabitants returned. Hoping to establish good relations from the start, Cortes ordered his men to be kind to the Indians. Bernal Diaz later wrote that the policy worked well:

> Men, women, and children, they went about among us as if they had been friendly with us all their lives, and Cortes ordered us not to harm them in

Cortes's Sacrifices for His King

Cortes sent five detailed letters to Spain's King Charles I describing his expedition to New Spain (Mexico). The first letter, compiled and sent by the council of Villa Rica de la Vera Cruz, published in Hernan Cortes: Letters from Mexico, *outlines the writer's sacrifices and Velasquez's stinginess.*

"While Diego Velazquez was . . . vexed on account of the little gold he had been brought, and eager to acquire more, he decided to gather a fleet and to send it. . . . So as to do it at somewhat less cost to himself, he spoke with Fernando [Hernando] Cortes . . . and suggested that between them they should fit out some eight or ten ships, for at that time Fernando Cortes was better equipped than anyone else on the island, having three ships of his own, and ready cash and being well thought of on the island. It was thought that many more people would follow him than anyone else, as in fact occurred. When Fernando Cortes heard what Diego Velazquez proposed he decided to spend his entire fortune in equipping a fleet and paid for nearly two-thirds of it, providing not only ships and supplies but also giving money to those who were to sail in the fleet but were unable to equip themselves . . . [for] the journey. . . . [Velasquez] contributed but a third of the cost."

HISTORIA
DE NUEVA-ESPAÑA,
ESCRITA POR SU ESCLARECIDO CONQUISTADOR
HERNAN CORTES,
AUMENTADA
CON OTROS DOCUMENTOS, Y NOTAS,
POR EL ILUSTRISSIMO SEÑOR
DON FRANCISCO ANTONIO
LORENZANA,
ARZOBISPO DE MEXICO.

OPIBUS CLARA, RELIGIONE NOBILIOR.

CON LAS LICENCIAS NECESARIAS.
En México en la Imprenta del Superior Gobierno, del Br. D. Joseph Antonio de Hogal en la Calle de Tiburcio. Año de 1770.

The title page of Historia de Nueva-España (History of New Spain), *a book which contains Cortes's correspondence to Spain's King Charles I.*

any way. Here in this island the Captain began to command most energetically, and Our Lord so favored him that whatever he touched succeeded, especially the pacification of the people.[10]

Cortes proved less diplomatic in spreading the Catholic faith. The Spanish soldiers found a temple filled with grimacing idols to which the natives offered human sacrifices. Cortes took the chiefs aside and told them idol worship and sacrifices were evil. After explaining Christianity to them, he urged them to destroy their idols and embrace the Catholic faith. The chiefs declined, saying that the Spaniards would all die at sea if they failed to respect the idols, the gods of the Indians' fathers.

Despite the local worshipers' resistance, Cortes ordered his men to cast down the idols from the temple that stood at the summit of a flat-topped pyramid. This done, the Spaniards built an altar on the site, set up an image of the Virgin Mary, and conducted a mass as the Indians watched from below. At the end of the mass, Cortes told the Indians that if they would worship the cross and keep it decorated with fresh flowers, they would prosper. The Indians promised to obey him.

The Spaniards forced Christianity on most of the Indian tribes that they came into contact with. Here Cortes orders his men to destroy an Indian idol and replace it with an image of the Virgin Mary.

Cortes Meets Aguilar

Having put the Indians' spiritual affairs in order, at least to his own satisfaction, Cortes prepared to leave for the mainland, but first he wanted news of other Europeans. When Cortes and his men first arrived on Cozumel, some of the islanders had shouted "Castilians, Castilians!" Knowing that other Spanish expeditions had touched the coasts of the western Caribbean, Cortes asked about other Caucasians in the area. Upon learning that some of his countrymen were being held as slaves on the mainland, he attempted to buy their freedom and bring them back to Cozumel. To this end, he gave some Indian messengers letters to deliver to the Spaniards and glass beads for ransom.

The ship returned with the news that the Indian messengers had found one Spaniard still alive. After they had purchased his freedom, the former captive asked to be allowed to bring the only other Spaniard in the area to join Cortes and said that he would meet the Spanish ship at the coastline for the trip to Cozumel. The crew waited for days, then abandoned hope of seeing the Spaniard again and re-

Conversion by Force

For centuries Spanish warriors had fought to reclaim Spain from the Moslems and to spread Catholicism. In Conquest of Mexico, *historian William H. Prescott explains Cortes's policy of conversion by force.*

"There was nothing which the Spanish government had more earnestly at heart, than the conversion of the Indians. It . . . gave . . . their military expeditions in this Western Hemisphere . . . the air of a crusade. The cavalier who embarked in them entered fully into these chivalrous and devotional feelings. [There was no] doubt . . . of the efficacy [effectiveness] of conversion, however sudden might be the change, or however violent the means. The sword was a good argument when the tongue failed; and the spread of Mohometanism [Islam] had shown that seeds sown by . . . violence, far from perishing in the ground, would spring up and bear fruit after time. . . . The war . . . to him . . . was a holy war. . . . The conversion of a single soul might cover a multitude of sins. . . . Such was the creed of the Castilian knight of the day. . . . No one partook more fully of [these] feelings than Hernando Cortes."

An illustration depicts the Spaniards' gruesome policy of conversion by force.

joined the rest of the fleet. Cortes ordered his fleet to sail for the mainland.

Shortly after their departure, Pedro de Alvarado's ship sprang a leak, forcing the fleet to return to Cozumel for repairs. While Cortes's men caulked the ship, a dark man dressed in rags, his hair cut like an Indian slave's, rowed his canoe ashore and approached them. Much to the crew's surprise, he spoke in clumsy Spanish. They took the stranger to Cortes, who gave him a change of clothes and questioned him.

The man, whose name was Jeronimo de Aguilar, had been shipwrecked in Yucatan along with seventeen other Spaniards eight years earlier. Two women in the group, he

Cortes in Cozumel

Accounts of historical events often conflict with each other. In The Conquest of New Spain, *Bernal Diaz writes that the Indians of Cozumel resisted conversion to Christianity. In* Cortes, *Gomora supplies a different version.*

"[The Indians] were pleased to have their idols cast down, and they even assisted at it, breaking into small pieces what they had formerly held sacred. And soon our Spaniards had left not a whole idol standing, and in each chapel they set up a Cross or the image of Our Lady [the Virgin Mary], whom all the islanders worshiped with prayer and great devotion, burning incense to her and offering partridges, maize, and fruits, and the other things they were accustomed to bring to their temples. Such was their devotion to the image of Our Lady that ever afterward, when Spanish ships touched at their island, they would run out to them shouting 'Cortes, Cortes!' and singing 'Maria, Maria!' Even more, they begged Cortes to leave someone behind to teach them to believe in the God of the Christians; but he did not dare consent, for fear they might kill the preacher, and also because he had few priests and friars with him. And in this he did wrong, in view of their earnest request."

told the captain-general, had been worked to death by the Indians. Some of the men had died of disease. Some had been sacrificed to the Indian idols. For a time the Indians had kept Aguilar in a wooden cage, where he was fattened in preparation for sacrifice, but he had escaped and become the slave of an Indian chief. There he had remained until the messengers sent by Cortes had ransomed him.

Aguilar had encouraged the other Spaniard, Gonzalo Guerrero, to come with him to join Cortes, but Guerrero refused. Guerrero had taken an Indian wife and lived according to Indian custom. The Indians now respected him as a leader in war. Aguilar added that when Spanish ships had arrived in Yucatan the year before, Guerrero had urged the Indians to drive them away before they could establish settlements on the coast. This news disturbed Cortes, who feared the renegade Spaniard's influence. Diaz later wrote that Cortes exclaimed "I wish I could get my hands on him. For it will never do to leave him here."[11]

On March 4, 1519, Cortes's fleet again sailed for Yucatan. Thanks to the delay, Cortes now had an interpreter who understood the Yucatan language. He also knew that a fellow Spaniard might rally the Indians against him and that if his men suffered defeat they would be offered to the gods of an unknown land.

Chapter

3 Into Battle

The clear blue Caribbean turned green just before it rolled onto the white sand beaches along the shores of Yucatan. A powerful gale from the north had torn at the ships all night, but now a rich, beautiful land lay before the Spaniards. Corn plantations abounded, and four large temples marked by tall statues of goddesses towered above the shoreline. Clearly the land was well populated.

The fleet followed the coast north to Champoton. Here both Cordova's and Grijalva's fleets had been attacked by natives and many Spaniards had been wounded and killed. Many of Cortes's men were veterans of those failed expeditions and hungered for revenge. The captain-general also wanted to avenge his countrymen's deaths, but his pilot, Anton de Alaminos, warned that the harbor offered the fleet little protection against shifting winds, which could batter the ships against the shore. So Cortes ordered the fleet northward along the coast.

Battle with the Tabascans

The fleet anchored at the Rio de Grijalva, called the Tabasco River by the natives. Juan de Grijalva had traded with the Indians here in 1518. Since the river was too shallow to accommodate the ships, Cortes ordered a detachment of men to row ashore in small boats. (Rowboats were used to put men and cargo ashore since seagoing vessels [ships] could not sail in shallow water.) As the conquistadors approached, thousands of warriors, their faces blackened with warpaint, lined the shores and filled the town (sometimes also called Tabasco). Some of the chiefs rowed along the shore in canoes shouting defiantly at the Spaniards. Cortes attempted to communicate that he wished to land peacefully to reprovision, and would give them until sundown to decide whether they would allow his party to come ashore.

The night passed without a reply from the Indians. Early the next morning, Cortes and his men heard mass together before they disembarked for the assault. Again Cortes offered peace to the Indians. Indeed, a Spanish law, the Requirement of 1513, obligated all conquistadors to warn native peoples that they would be attacked if they resisted. While the Indians probably understood little of Cortes's speech, it was clear that the Spanish soldiers were invaders. Seeing the white men's small numbers, the Indians laughed at the warning and stood ready for battle.

Crying "Sant' Iago!" ("Saint James!") as they advanced, the conquistadors waded ashore through a hail of Indian arrows and javelins. After a bitter struggle, the Spaniards advanced to the center of the town. There Cortes made three cuts on a large tree as a sign that he claimed the land in the name of King Charles I. Some of Velasquez's followers complained that Cortes should have claimed the land in Velasquez's name, since the governor had appointed Cortes as the expedition leader. It was a sign of things to come.

The conquistadors encountered a hail of arrows and javelins as they disembarked on the Rio de Grijalva coast in the Yucatan.

Night fell, ending the fighting, but the Indians renewed their assault the next morning. For days the fighting continued. Each side held advantages. The Spaniards, with their crossbows, cannon, matchlock muskets, and steel swords, inflicted fearful casualties on the natives. Despite the introduction of new and terrible weapons, the natives courageously pressed their attack.

On March 25, 1519, Cortes landed his horses and led the small cavalry in a surprise attack on the Indians while his foot soldiers engaged them as well. Four hundred Spanish infantry faced forty thousand Indian warriors, a colorful mass arrayed in plumed battle dress. Cortes and a handful of other riders reached the battlefield unseen by the Indians, approaching the defenders from behind. The charge began.

Weapons of Terror

Horses were unknown in Yucatan. The Indians saw horse and rider as one creature and thought they were seeing huge animals with two heads. Many warriors believed that horses fed on human flesh. Despite the bravery of the native troops in the face of small arm and cannon fire, wherever the cavalry appeared, the Indians were driven back. Once, as the Indians and Cortes's foot soldiers fought desperately, a single cavalryman on a dapple-gray horse appeared, and the warriors fled in terror. Many of the soldiers thought Saint James had miraculously come to their aid from heaven. Cortes believed the horseman had been his patron, Saint Peter. Inspired by the rider, the soldiers drove the Indians from the battlefield.

The Indians, who had never seen a horse, were filled with terror at the sight of the Spanish warriors on horseback. Believing the horse and rider to be one creature, the Indians fled from the two-headed beasts.

When the Battle of Cintla (as the Spaniards called it) ended, as many as eight hundred Indian dead littered the battlefield. Although the Indians had fought fiercely and wounded many Spaniards, only two of the attackers had died. The Tabascan chiefs agreed to a peace conference.

By now Cortes realized that he could use horses and cannon to intimidate the chiefs at the upcoming meetings. He instructed his men to load their largest cannon and be ready to fire at a prearranged signal. Then he had a mare in heat tied overnight at the place he intended to stand when he spoke to the chiefs. The following morning, Cortes's men took the mare away, but her scent remained.

When the chiefs arrived, Cortes berated them for resisting his landing. The fighting and deaths had been their fault,

The Requirement of 1513

In reading the Requirement of 1513 to the Indians, the Spanish government was attempting to protect the rights of conquered people; however, the probable result was confusion. Historian Paul Horgan explains the process in Conquistadors in North American History.

"Before hostilities, and upon a command from the Captain General, the royal notary would produce . . . the Requirement of 1513 from which he would formally read aloud . . . those conditions upon which . . . the Spanish could legally offer battle.

The Requirement opened with a brief sketch of the history of the world. It then moved on to a discussion of the papacy . . . for in 1493 Pope Alexander VI had assigned ownership of any lands discovered in the Western hemisphere to Spain and Portugal.

The ritual . . . continued with a demand that the Indians yield themselves to the Spanish Crown and accept . . . Christianity. If . . . they should agree, then no hostilities would follow. If . . . they should resist, then 'with fire and sword' the newcomers would impose their will."

The Conquistadors' Weapons

Spanish weapons technology in 1519 was thousands of years ahead of that of the conquistadors' Indian adversaries. In Cortes, *Gomara describes the natives' amazement at having been conquered by a handful of men.*

"They said they considered themselves a mighty people . . . because nobody dared to take their goods and women by force, or their children for sacrifice. This was their thought when they saw those few strangers, but they had been greatly undeceived when they measured their strength against them. . . . Besides, they had been dazzled by the flashing swords, . . . and they found the roar and flames of the guns more stunning than thunder and lightning from the skies. . . . They also were astonished and frightened by the horses, whose great mouths seemed about to swallow them, and also by the speed with which the horses overtook them. . . . Since they had never before seen a horse, the first one that attacked them terrified them . . . and when it was joined by many more, they could not stand against the shock and strength and fury of their charge."

Artist Frederic Remington drew this illustration of a Spanish conquistador on a horse. These animals proved to be one of the Spaniards' most effective weapons against the Indians.

he said, for the Spaniards had come peacefully as the vassals (servants) of the greatest ruler on earth, Charles I of Spain. He assured them that Charles was prepared to offer good treatment to all who entered his service. Those who resisted would be killed. The big guns, he warned, were still angry with the Indians. (Cortes suspected that the Indians thought the cannon were living beings and encour-

Cortes's men used cannon like this bronze breech-loader to frighten and subdue the Indians, who believed that the artillery were living beings.

aged the belief.) Bernal Diaz, who was present when Cortes told the chiefs that the cannon would kill them, describes the incident in his chronicle of the conquest:

> [Cortes said] some of those [cannon] were still angry at them for having attacked us. At this moment he secretly gave the order for the loaded cannon to be fired, and it went off with the requisite thunderous report, the ball whistling away over the hills. . . . The Caciques [chiefs] were thoroughly terrified.[12]

Cortes's men then led a stallion to the place where the mare had been tied. Facing the chiefs, the stallion sniffed the earth, picked up the mare's scent, and began to neigh loudly, pawing the ground and rearing. Already unnerved by the cannon, the chiefs were still more terrified by the horse's display. Cortes ordered the stallion led away and told the chiefs that the horse had scolded him for failing to punish the Indians who had attacked Spanish soldiers. The trembling chiefs quickly pledged their loyalty to Charles and his representatives, begged the forgiveness of all the horses, and offered them turkeys and roses to eat. Throughout the conquest, Cortes shrewdly evaluated his enemies and devised effective techniques of intimidation.

Marina

On the next morning the chiefs returned bearing gifts and bringing the population of the town, as Cortes had ordered. The chiefs offered twenty women to Cortes and his men. Among them was a dark-eyed beauty named Malinche, the daughter of a chief in the Aztec realm. Having been sold into slavery in Yucatan she knew the languages of the Aztecs and the Mayans.

Malinche (later christened Marina by a Spanish priest) became Cortes's trusted adviser. Whenever he spoke to the natives of Mexico, Aguilar and Marina stood by his side. Cortes found he could communicate by speaking Spanish to Aguilar, who then spoke in Mayan to Malinche. In turn, Malinche translated from Mayan to Aztec. Marina, who served as the captain-general's eyes and ears, more than once warned Cortes of plots to destroy the little army and suggested strategies to exploit the natives' superstitions. So closely were the two associated that the Indians began to call Cortes Malinche, too. For a time, Doña Marina became Cortes's mistress, and she bore his favorite son, Martin.

Knowing that some of the Indian women might become wives to the soldiers, Cortes used the occasion to convert the chiefs and all their people to Christianity. He invited the chiefs to destroy their idols and abandon the practice of human sacrifice. By now anxious to cooperate with the invaders, the chiefs agreed, and with the help of Spanish carpenters erected a large cross and an altar.

While Cortes and his men remained in Tabasco, the Indians supplied food in large quantities and continued to bring

Tabascan chiefs make a peace offering of twenty female slaves to Cortes. Among the women was Marina, who became Cortes's mistress and valuable translator.

A Valuable Adviser

Without Aguilar and Marina, Cortes's expedition might have ended in disaster. In A History of Latin America, from the Beginnings to the Present, *historian Hubert Herring emphasizes Marina's importance to Cortes.*

"Malinche—Cortes's mistress, counselor, interpreter—rendered as great service as any hundred fighting men. Time and again her quick wit saved Cortes from torture and death. Out of love for her master, she told what she knew of Moctezuma's empire, of its vastness and great population and the bitter wars between subject tribes. She told Cortes of the superstitions of priests and rulers, of the legend of long-lost Quetzalcoatl, the fabulous god-king who had promised to return out of the waters of the East. She told of the astrologers who were convinced by heavenly signs that the white strangers in their white-winged ships were the invincible army of Quetzalcoatl. Malinche herself may have believed that her lover and master was indeed that gracious and all-powerful god and king."

gifts to the conquerors. In addition to food, they brought some cloth, Indian masks, and golden objects, including diadems, small figurines, and sandals. The items were of small value, but Cortes questioned the Indians about the source of their gold. They replied that they had little of the yellow metal, which they neither mined nor considered particularly valuable. When Cortes asked them again where the gold came from, the Tabascans pointed west toward the towering mountains, the Sierra de Tamaulipas, and said "Mexico." Immediately, according to Gomara, Cortes decided to march inland to the land where gold was found:

> This account convinced Cortes that that land was not for the Spaniards, and that it was not a place to make a settlement, there being no gold or silver or other treasure in it, so he decided to advance into the western country where the gold was.[13]

Chapter

4 The Return of the Gods

As the fleet sailed along the east coast of Central America, veterans of Grijalva's expedition pointed out the landmarks and told of their adventures in each place. Finally, on the Thursday before Easter, 1519, Cortes's pilot, Alaminos, guided the ships into a harbor well protected from the fierce gales common to the region. The landing site, called San Juan de Ulua by the Spaniards, lies just north of modern-day Veracruz.

Before the Spanish soldiers disembarked, Indians rowed from the shore in two large canoes, boarded Cortes's flagship, and asked to see the Spanish chief. Marina led them to Cortes. Announcing that they came in the name of Montezuma, the ambassadors began to dress Cortes in feather robes, jade, and gold—the clothing of an Aztec god.

Seeing that the Indians revered him, Cortes took the opportunity to intimidate the delegation and asked if this was all they had brought him. When the Indians answered that they had nothing else to offer, Cortes had them shackled. As the emissaries stood on the ship's deck in chains, Cortes ordered a cannon fired. All the Indians passed out, terrified. At Cortes's command, the Spaniards revived and released the Indians, who fled to their boats and quickly paddled away.

A detail from an embroidered cloth depicts Cortes and Marina disembarking at San Juan de Ulua on Good Friday.

Cortes accepts gifts from Aztec envoys sent by Montezuma. At his side, Marina translates the Indians' language and signs.

By the time Cortes landed his men on the next day, Good Friday, the Aztec messengers were well on their way to Montezuma in the Aztec capital, Tenochtitlan, which was also called Mexico. (The name "Mexico" was used, as well, to designate the lands surrounding the city.) Three days later, two Indian nobles and four thousand unarmed Indians arrived at the Spanish camp bringing gifts of food and gold. The nobles, one of whom was named Teudilli, told Cortes that they, too, were the servants of Montezuma. Greeting them in friendly fashion, Cortes gave them more glass beads and explained that his master, the greatest king on earth, Charles I of Spain, wanted the captain-general to visit Montezuma, about whom he had heard so much.

Then he fired his cannon and had his cavalry gallop and maneuver to impress his guests with Spanish power. Though unnerved by the display of military might, the Aztec nobles instructed their scribes to paint images of all they had seen on cotton cloth. After all, were they not the eyes and ears of the great king Montezuma?

A helmeted Spanish soldier walked past the Aztecs, arresting Teudilli's attention. The Indian nobleman told Cortes that the helmet resembled one left to his people by their ancestors and now resting on the head of a statue representing the god Huitzilopochtli in Tenochtitlan. The observant Teudilli asked Cortes if he might take the helmet to show Montezuma. The captain-general granted the request but asked that the helmet be returned filled with gold. This would permit Cortes to compare Aztec gold to the gold found in Spanish streams. The Indian nobleman agreed to forward the request to Montezuma and left for the capital.

Cortes Is Considered a God

During one visit by the Aztec emissaries to the Spanish camp, the Indians sacrificed human victims in the conquistadors' presence, soaked maize (corn) cakes in the resulting blood, and offered them to the Spaniards as food. Sickened by the gesture, Cortes did not realize that Montezuma was testing the Spaniards to see whether they were gods or men. The Aztecs believed that a god would eat human flesh and blood.

Each time white men appeared on the coast, Montezuma feared the visitation might be the fulfillment of a prophecy: Aztec legend held that the greatest of the people's gods, Quetzalcoatl, had left Mexico in ancient times and would return to reclaim his kingdom. When the god reap-

A stone sculpture representing the Aztec god Quetzalcoatl. Montezuma mistook Cortes for the god, who according to legend would come from the east in the form of a white-skinned man.

peared, he would come as a white-skinned man and would arrive from the east, across the sea—from the land where the sun rises.

For ten years, the Aztecs had seen omens, signs of the god's return, and each new omen filled Montezuma's heart with dread. While Caucasians had reached Yucatan's shores before, never had they come when all the signs appeared. Never had they scattered Indian warriors like leaves before a storm. This particular solar cycle, which the Spaniards called the year 1519, had been foretold as the time the god would return. Now the ambassadors showed Montezuma the painted pictures of travelers from the east, bearded men with fair skin who made the earth shake and heavens roar. The mightiest ruler in the Americas trembled.

Within seven days, Teudilli returned accompanied by one hundred Indian bearers carrying gifts that stunned the Spaniards. After scenting Cortes with costly incense, a ritual reserved for a god, the Aztecs presented the Spanish commander with the helmet Teudilli had taken, filled with fine gold. Then Indian bearers brought Cortes two disks as large as cartwheels, one of silver carved to represent the moon and one of solid gold carved in the image of the sun. Having seen these tantalizing samples of Montezuma's wealth, Cortes could not be discouraged by any force from entering Tenochtitlan. The Aztecs, however, stated firmly that Cortes and his Spaniards were to remain on the coast where the Indians could feed them and bring them more gifts.

Debate on the subject ended when the vesper bell rang, calling the Europeans to worship. The Aztec nobles asked why the Spaniards bowed before an oddly cut tree (the cross). Cortes explained Christianity to them, urging the Indians to accept the faith. Cortes then gave the Aztec ambassadors a small picture of the Virgin Mary and the Christ child. The nobles reluctantly accepted the image and returned to their quarters.

Cortes Gains Allies

When Cortes arose the next morning, all the Indians had left the encampment. Without servants to gather or prepare food, the little army's welfare was threatened. Fearing the Indians' sudden disappearance might signal an attack, Cortes ordered his men to be more vigilant than ever.

Aztec Origins

When Cortes reached Mexico, the warlike Aztecs had been militarily powerful for two centuries. In The American Indian, *Anne Terry White and William Brandon describe Aztec origins.*

"About the middle of the 13th century there wandered into the Valley of Mexico a rude tribe of spearmen who called themselves the Mexica. They hired themselves out as mercenaries at first and, having no land of their own, settled on a miserable little group of islands in Lake Texcoco. They named their dwelling place Tenochtitlan (Place of the Cactus-in-the-Rock).

They prospered. Little by little their town grew. . . . When a hundred years had passed, it was one of the two chief cities in the entire country.

By this time the people . . . called themselves . . . Aztecs, for their legends said their original home had been a place called Aztlan. They had also chosen for their very own a suitable god—Huitzilopochtli (Weet-seel-o-poch-tlee), 'omen of evil, creator of war.' It was this god who told them . . . they were his chosen people and would rule the world. The Aztecs proceeded to do so, so far as Mexico was concerned."

An illustration depicts the legendary founding of Tenochtitlan. The Aztecs believed that they were the chosen people destined to rule the world.

As Cortes pondered his next step, several Indians entered the camp. They said they had come from the city of Cempoala and had not approached before because Aztecs had been present. Now the Cempoalan chief and people announced their wish to serve Cortes. Marina then told Cortes that many of the towns in the region paid tribute to Montezuma only because they feared the Aztec armies. Cempoala was one of these towns. The news that Aztec domination depended on terror delighted Cortes, for he realized that the Indians could be turned against one another. Shrewdly, Cortes planned to use the ancient strategy of divide and conquer. He concluded that God had placed a powerful weapon in his hands.

Cortes Founds Villa Rica de la Vera Cruz

As Cortes became more determined to enter Mexico, greed and fear made many of his men anxious to turn back. Thanks to the Aztec ambassadors' visits, the Spaniards had already acquired more wealth than they had ever hoped to see, and many were anxious to return to Cuba while they were ahead. Velasquez's supporters demanded that Cortes obey the governor's orders to engage only in trading and return immediately. Cortes's orders, they argued, gave him no authority to establish a colony anywhere in the new land. Even Velasquez possessed no such authority.

Drawing on his legal training, Cortes conspired with his supporters to end his dependence on Velasquez's authority. The men voted to establish a fortified town on the coast of Mexico north of Yucatan. They agreed to call the new settlement Villa Rica de la Vera Cruz (Rich Village of the True Cross), formed a town council, and elected Cortes captain-general (military commander) for the town. Under Spanish law, these acts left Cortes answerable directly to King Charles and authorized him to establish colonies in the new land.

Pretending reluctance, Cortes accepted the position and the council's offer

Aztec ambassadors urged Cortes not to enter Tenochtitlan. However, the endless supply of gold and fine gifts that they presented to him only reinforced his desire to conquer the city.

Montezuma Tests the White Men

Bernardino de Sahagun was a sixteenth-century Spanish friar who compiled a history of the conquest. Fray Bernardino's multivolume work, which was translated from the Spanish by Arthur J.O. Anderson and Charles E. Dibble, explains that Montezuma had instructed his first messengers to treat the white men as gods.

"And he sent the . . . brave [warriors] to secure all the food [the Spaniards] would need. . . . And . . . they were to look to them well. He sent captives so that . . . [they] would drink their blood. . . .

But when [the Spaniards] beheld this, much were they nauseated. They spat; they closed their eyes tight . . . , they shook their heads. And [the Aztecs] had soaked . . . food in blood. . . . Much did it revolt them; it nauseated them.

And Moctezuma had acted thus because he thought them gods. . . . They were called . . . 'gods come from heaven. . . .'

For this reason did Moctezuma send the magicians . . . that they might see of what sort [the Spaniards] were; that they might . . . use their wizardry upon them, cast a spell over them . . . so that they might take sick, might die, or else because of it turn back.

But . . . they . . . could do nothing [against the Spaniards]."

of one-fifth of all goods acquired, an amount equal to the king's share, to repay his expenses in outfitting the expedition. Several of Velasquez's supporters, sensing intrigue and fearing for their lives, insisted that the expedition return to Cuba. On the captain-general's command, they were put under arrest. Then, according to Diaz, Cortes gained the support of his less outspoken opponents through persuasion, flattery, and bribery:

> As Cortes was most energetic in every direction, he managed to make friends with the partisans of Diego Velasquez, for, with that solvent of hardness, presents of gold from our store to some, and promises to others, he brought them over to his side, . . . took them out of prison . . . after a few days, and made good friends of them . . . all through gold![14]

Cortes in Cempoala

As the army moved up the coast to build the new town at a site with a better harbor, some Cempoalans invited Cortes and his men to come to their town. The chief of Cempoala, dubbed "the Fat Cacique" by

The magnificent city of Tenochtitlan as it might have looked before being ravaged by the Spanish conquerors.

the Spanish soldiers, greeted Cortes warmly and complained that the Aztecs demanded gold and silver as tribute, took their most beautiful women for Montezuma's harem, and sacrificed their people to the gods. Cortes listened with special interest to the Fat Cacique's description of Tenochtitlan, its location on a lake, its mighty defenses, its huge armies, and its great wealth. At the chief's suggestion, Cortes formed a military alliance with Cempoala and began to recruit other Indian cities to his cause.

In one city, Aztec collectors arrived while the Spanish soldiers were present and demanded payment of tribute to Montezuma. Cortes persuaded the chiefs of the town to arrest the collectors. Then, without the chiefs' knowledge, he released the collectors, who had surely expcted to be executed, and sent them with messages of friendship to Montezuma. Thus by tricking his hosts into angering the Aztecs, Cortes had made the Cempoalans dependent on his protection, and at the same time made Montezuma less willing to attack the Spaniards. Gomara wrote admiringly of Cortes's strategy:

> Cortes' thought was to stir these people up in order to win them and their lands over to his support, seeing that without them he could accomplish little. He had the constables arrested; released them; made new overtures to Moctezuma; aroused the town and the country roundabout; and left them in rebellion so that they should have need of him.[15]

With the region aligned behind him, Cortes returned with Cempoalan laborers to build Villa Rica, including a stockade that contained a church, an armory, and a gallows. After the fortress was completed, more Aztec emissaries arrived. The visitors, who included relatives of Montezuma, brought the usual gifts for Cortes and thanked him for saving the tribute collectors. To the stunned Cempoalans it seemed that Montezuma was paying Cortes tribute. The Indians' reaction was not lost on Diaz:

> These towns of the sierra [the Tamaulipas mountain chain] . . . and . . . Cempoala had hitherto been very much afraid of the Mexicans. . . . When they saw the kinsmen of the great Montezuma arriving with presents . . . and paying marked respect to Cortes . . .

> they were fairly astounded. . . . The Caciques said to one another that we must be Teules [gods] for Montezuma had fear of us. . . . If we already had reputation for valour, from this time forth it was greatly increased.[16]

Anxious to strengthen his alliance with the powerful strangers, the Fat Cacique offered the Spaniards a number of Indian maidens as wives. Cortes explained that his men could not marry the women nor fully accept the Cempoalans as brothers unless they became Christians and cast down their idols. The Fat Cacique politely refused, saying that the gods would punish them all if the sacred temples were defiled.

With anger rising in their hearts, the soldiers listened to the chief's defense of what they considered devil worship. During their stay in Cempoala, the soldiers had discovered that in rituals the Cempoalans sacrificed and devoured four or five people daily. None of the Spaniards wanted the carnage to continue. Cortes shouted to his men that they could not permit such crimes against God.

To the Cempoalans' horror, the soldiers scrambled up to the top of the temple and sent the idols crashing down the steps. Warriors drew their bows to defend their gods, but the Fat Cacique suddenly found himself at the point of a Spanish sword. Warned by Cortes that he and his priests would die if the warriors attacked, the terrified chief ordered his men not to resist. As the Indians stood among the fragments of their idols, they concluded that their gods were powerless before the Christians, accepted the new religion, and built a cross on their temple. Afterward, the Cempoalans remained loyal to Cortes.

Cortes Destroys His Ships

When Cortes returned to Villa Rica, he learned that a ship had arrived from Cuba bringing two horses, ten men, and the news that the king had authorized Velasquez to establish settlements in Mexico. Anxious to make good his claim to the

Aghast at the human sacrifice practiced by the Cempoalans, Cortes and his men topple the Indians' idols.

Cortes orders his ships dismantled to prevent mutiny among his army, leaving the soldiers little choice but to assist in the conquest or risk death.

land he now called New Spain, Cortes loaded a ship with treasure and sent it to Charles with a letter explaining his activities in New Spain. Four days after the ship left, Cortes discovered that several of his own men who were supporters of Velasquez planned to commandeer a ship, kill its pilot, sail to Cuba, and arrange for Velasquez to intercept the treasure ship.

Conquistadors were always difficult to control and their captain-generals' powers were limited, but Cortes could not tolerate mutiny. He had the conspirators interrogated until they confessed, whereupon a trial was held. Cortes ordered two men hanged and several flogged; one man's feet were cut off, a virtual death sentence. The captain-general loudly protested his reluctance to impose these punishments, but the message was clear. Velasquez's followers could not safely oppose Cortes.

To avoid further treachery, Cortes secretly persuaded his ships' pilots to spread the rumor that the vessels were rotten and unseaworthy. He then ordered all the ships but one unloaded and dismantled, saving only the sails, rigging, and ironwork. Those who wished to return to Cuba could sail on the remaining ship with his blessing, he added. A number accepted this offer, saying they would rather go home than die fighting the Indian hordes. Having lured his opponents into the open, Cortes ordered the last ship dismantled as well. Now the tiny band, with no means of escape and its back to the sea, had little choice but to conquer the land or die.

Chapter 5 Tlaxcala

As the captain-general prepared to march on Mexico, Spanish ships arrived at Villa Rica. With his right to colonize Mexico in question, Cortes regarded even Spanish ships with suspicion. A landing party came ashore from the vessels only to be captured by the captain-general's men. The captured Spaniards told Cortes that Francisco de Garay, the Spanish governor of the Caribbean island of Jamaica, had sent the expedition to claim Mexico. With persuasive words, a few bribes of Indian gold, and the promise of riches beyond their wildest dreams, Cortes quickly recruited the captives to his service. By now wary of Cortes's tricks, Garay and his men sailed away. For the moment the captain-general had discouraged a competitor for glory and gold.

Clearly, Tenochtitlan was the storehouse of that Indian gold. Cortes left some soldiers at Villa Rica and instructed his Indian allies to help them complete the buildings. As protection against Indian rebellion, the captain-general took some chiefs with him—officially, to act as guides; unofficially, they were hostages. Cortes accepted the Cempoalans' advice and traveled to Tenochtitlan through Tlaxcala, a mountain republic whose people hated the Aztecs and had remained independent of them for generations.

The Mountain People

On August 16, 1519, Cortes's little army moved inland. Finding the Indians' footpaths too narrow and overgrown to accommodate horses and cannon, the Spaniards hacked their way over mountains and through valleys. At times the growth was so dense that cities inhabited by thousands of Indians seemed to arise out of nowhere.

In each city the chiefs spoke reverently of Montezuma's greatness. One chief, seeing the white-skinned, bearded Cortes, asked the Cempoalans if the strangers were the gods from the east. By now convinced of Cortes's divinity, the Cempoalans proudly answered that these were the white-skinned gods of legend. Along the road to Tlaxcala, the Indians gave the presumed gods gifts of gold but apologized for the smallness of their offerings, explaining that the Aztecs had collected the rest as tribute. The hand of Montezuma could be seen everywhere. Thousands of Aztec troops garrisoned the towns along the road, and Aztec runners carried messages in relays to Tenochtitlan at a speed that amazed Cortes. Earlier, Cortes had written King Charles boasting that he planned to capture Montezuma.

Montezuma's power extended far beyond the boundaries of Tenochtitlan. While Cortes was intent on capturing the wealth and power of the great ruler, he realized that it would not be an easy task.

Now the sights he saw as he neared Tenochtitlan convinced him the task ahead would prove more challenging than he had imagined. Gomara later wrote that Cortes concealed his doubts well:

> Up to this point Cortes had not entirely realized the wealth and power of Moctezuma, although he anticipated many obstacles, difficulties, dangers, and other things on his way thither—even so, when he heard all this, which would have dismayed many brave men, he showed no sign of faltering; rather, the more marvels he heard of that great lord, the greater his desire to see him.[17]

The little army marched higher into the cool air of the mountains, where a new obstacle lay across their path. Spanning a huge valley between peaks stood a stone wall, nine feet tall and over fifty wide, which clearly had been built to keep out invaders. The Spanish soldiers had reached the frontier of Tlaxcala.

The army threaded its way through a mazelike opening in the wall and continued its march. Cortes sent three Indian messengers ahead to tell the Tlaxcalans of their peaceful intentions, and in a few days they returned with a reply. By now, the Tlaxcalans had heard of Montezuma's gifts to the white men and had decided that Cortes was an ally of the Aztecs. They arranged a response to the peace offer that could not be misinterpreted: On September 5, 1519, six thousand Tlaxcalans attacked Cortes's army.

The Indians showered the advancing Spanish troops with arrows and fire-hardened spears, and, unlike most of the native warriors the Europeans had met so far, the Tlaxcalans showed no fear. Arrows, javelins, and stones from slings lay deep on the ground as the Spaniards continued their advance. Knowing that defeat meant death on the altar block if not on the battlefield, the conquistadors fought desperately. Soldiers no longer bothered to aim cannon or muskets. Any shot, no matter how carelessly placed, found a target among the densely packed warriors. Fear mounted in the Spaniards' hearts. They had expected the Tlaxcalans to welcome them as allies, but had found enemies, instead.

Daily the conquistadors' situation worsened. Weakened by fever, at times Cortes was unable to lead in battle, and most of the soldiers had been wounded. Faced with what seemed a hopeless situation, Cortes relied as much on bluff as on his men's sword arms. He ordered forty-five soldiers who had died of wounds buried secretly so the Tlaxcalans would believe they had killed no Spaniards. When the Aztec ambassadors arrived in his camp during the campaign, he boldly told them to stay and see the Spaniards defeat Montezuma's enemies.

Cortes also used simple terror. Knowing that all things remaining equal, the Tlaxcalans' huge numbers would eventually overwhelm the Spaniards, he gambled on bringing the campaign to a speedy conclusion by aggressive action. He and his men began raiding Indian cities, at times killing women and children. At the same time, he sent messengers to the enemy with a grim warning: Make peace or Spanish troops will ravage the lands and destroy Tlaxcala, the main city.

The threat was well timed. To the Tlaxcalans it seemed that the Spaniards were supermen—the Europeans anticipated their plans, fought successfully when vastly outnumbered, and struck down seasoned warriors with thunder. Tlaxcala's chiefs met and decided to accept Cortes's peace offer and offer him their allegiance. At the chiefs' invitation, on September 18, 1519, Cortes led his victorious army into Tlaxcala itself.

Remarkably, the people who had done everything in their power to destroy the Spaniards now welcomed them into their city. Everywhere, the conquistadors found food and comfortable lodging. They also found captives in cages being fattened for sacrifice. Cortes ordered the release of these prisoners, a policy he continued throughout his Mexican campaign.

After his men had rested and recovered from their wounds, Cortes continued

Upon their entry into Tlaxcala, Cortes's army is attacked by a horde of warriors, six thousand strong. After more than a week of bloody fighting, Tlaxcalan chiefs accepted a peace offer and swore their allegiance to Cortes.

the advance into Mexico. The Tlaxcalan chiefs sent warriors and hostages with Cortes to prove their loyalty to their new ally. Now in command of a combined Spanish-Indian army, the captain-general led his army toward Cholula, a city loyal to Montezuma and the legendary home of the god Quetzalcoatl. The Tlaxcalans begged Cortes to choose another route, warning him of the likelihood of an Aztec ambush. As always, the captain-general kept his men under arms day and night, alert to possible surprise attack.

Massacre at Cholula

The road to Cholula took Cortes's army out of the cool mountains and across a bleak high desert. One long stretch, blackened by lava, offered no comfort to man or beast. At last they saw Cholula, its white temples rising out of a green valley surrounded by dusty plains. Cholulan nobles, dressed in gaudy, feathered robes, marched out of the city to welcome the Spanish army. Leaving his Tlaxcalan auxiliaries outside the city to avoid conflict between traditional enemies, Cortes and his men entered Cholula. Thousands of citizens lined the streets and rooftops to catch a glimpse of the newcomers. For two days the Cholulans supplied the Spaniards' every need.

Then two Aztec ambassadors arrived from Tenochtitlan. Abruptly, the Cholulans' attitude changed. They stopped supplying adequate food to the Spanish soldiers and spoke disrespectfully to them. Cortes also noticed that the Cholulans had stockpiled stones on the rooftops, and

The Officers Encourage Cortes

Many of Cortes's men became more afraid to enter Mexico after they had fought the Tlaxcalans. In his account, Diaz credited the army's officers with encouraging both the soldiers and their commander.

"We began to wonder what would be the outcome of all this fighting. . . . To march into Mexico we thought too arduous an undertaking because of its great armies, and we said to one another that if those Tlaxcalans . . . could reduce us to these straits, what would happen when we found ourselves at war with the great forces of Montezuma?. . . As there were among us very excellent gentlemen and soldiers, . . . Cortes never said or did anything [important] without first asking advice. . . .

One and all we put heart into Cortes, and told him that . . . with the help of God we had escaped from such perilous battles, our Lord Jesus Christ must have preserved us for some good end."

With the help of their Tlaxcalan allies, Cortes's army massacred Cholulans by the thousands and took control of the city in a matter of minutes.

women and children had disappeared from the streets as if evacuated. In addition, the Spaniards found in the streets pits lined with sharpened stakes, concealed by flimsy matting.

Marina soon confirmed Cortes's fears, warning that the Aztecs had ordered the Cholulans to trap the Spaniards in the city and annihilate them when they continued their march to Tenochtitlan. Worse still, an army of twenty thousand Aztecs lurked outside the city to ambush any who might escape. According to the plan, the Cholulans were to kill all but twenty Spaniards, who would be sacrificed to the gods. Quietly, Cortes brought some Cholulan nobles in for questioning, and they confirmed Marina's report. Cortes acted quickly. He informed the Cholulan chiefs that his army would leave for Tenochtitlan the next morning and asked them to supply Indian bearers according to local custom. Then he ordered his Tlaxcalan allies to prepare for battle.

When morning came, the Cholulan chiefs, nobles, and bearers met Cortes and his men in the city's plaza. Accusing the Cholulans of treachery, Cortes and his men drew their swords and mowed down surprised Cholulans by the thousands. Those who tried to force their way into the plaza to help their countrymen found soldiers firing cannon from every entryway and Tlaxcalan warriors slashing and stabbing at them from behind. In minutes, the holy city of Cholula was in the Spaniards' hands.

Triumphant Tlaxcalans rushed to loot the city and enslave their hereditary enemies, as Cortes gathered the surviving Cholulan nobles and the Aztec ambassadors. Angrily, he told them the city deserved to be destroyed, but he would spare it out of respect for Montezuma.

Then, much to the amazement of the defeated Cholulans, Cortes ordered the Tlaxcalans to return all they had stolen and free their captives. Hereafter, he commanded, the people of Cholula and Tlaxcala would be brothers.

Accustomed to seeing victors cannibalize the vanquished, the Indians were amazed at Cortes's combination of vengeance and leniency. Although Cortes's actions would be called brutal by twentieth-century standards, his use of terror tactics probably encouraged many Indians to submit to him, avoiding further bloodshed. Word of the Cholulan massacre spread rapidly throughout the region, and with it a growing legend of Cortes's ability to read his enemies' minds. Diaz believed that this superstition intimidated the Indians and protected the Spanish:

> This affair and punishment at Cholula became known throughout the provinces of New Spain, and if we had a reputation for valour before, from now on they took us for sorcerers, and said that no evil that was planned against us could be so hidden from us that it did not come to our knowledge, and on this account they showed us good will.[18]

The View from the Volcano

With the Cholulans subdued, the army of Cortes began to march to Tenochtitlan, which lay roughly fifty miles to the west. Throughout the journey, the people of town after town offered Cortes their loyalty and asked his protection against the Aztecs. As always, he assured the natives that his king had sent him to protect the oppressed and bring justice to the land.

After a few days, the Spanish soldiers climbed into the mountains, where bitter winds cut through their ragged clothes.

Indians watch in amazement as Spanish soldiers attempt to scale the dangerously hot slopes of the Popocateptl volcano.

Montezuma Offers Cortes Bribes

After Cortes and his men defeated the Tlaxcalans, Montezuma tried to keep the Spaniards of Mexico away by offering bribes, swearing loyalty to the Spanish king, and by lame excuses. In his second letter to Charles I, Cortes told of the Aztec king's strategy.

"Six chieftains of rank, vassals of Mutezuma [Montezuma], came to see me with as many as two hundred men in attendance. They told me that they had come on behalf of Mutezuma to inform me how he wished to be Your Highness's vassal and my ally, and that I should say what I wished him to pay as an annual tribute to Your Highness in gold and silver and jewels as well as slaves, cotton, clothing, and other things which he possessed; all of which he would give, provided that I did not go to his land, the reason being that it was very barren and lacking in all provisions and it would grieve him if I and those who came with me should be in want. . . .

They made many . . . attempts to cause trouble between me and [the Tlaxcalans], saying they were not speaking the truth nor was the friendship they offered me sincere. . . . The people of [Tlaxcala], on the other hand warned me many times not to trust Mutezuma's vassals for . . . everything they did was done with treachery."

In the distance, they could see the twin peaks of the volcanoes, Ixtaccihuatl and Popocateptl towering over three miles above sea level. Both volcanoes had become far more active than usual in the year Cortes and his men arrived in Mexico, and most Indians considered this an evil omen. Visibly nervous, the Indians warned Cortes that no mortal could climb the smoldering summits and live. A few soldiers, encouraged by Cortes to accept the challenge, scaled the slopes nearing the craters and returned with huge icicles as proof of their adventure. Cortes never tired of reminding the Indians that no task was too great for a Spaniard.

Passing west between the two peaks, the conquistadors suddenly beheld the Valley of Mexico. A patchwork of orderly fields stretched across the great basin. In the center of the valley lay Lake Texcoco, a great blue gem shimmering on an emerald carpet. Roads connecting towns formed slim lines and crossed the lake. The lines met at one gleaming white point—Tenochtitlan.

Chapter

6 The Land of Enchantment

Viewed through the clear mountain air, Tenochtitlan seemed close at hand, but it still lay two days' march away. Their destination in sight, Cortes's men headed toward the valley in high spirits, but man-made obstacles slowed the army's progress. The Aztecs had strewn trees and boulders across the road to discourage Cortes from taking what they claimed was a dangerous route to the capital. Suspecting that the Aztecs intended to ambush his men on a more accessible, supposedly safer road, Cortes ignored the advice and had his Tlaxcalan allies clear a path.

Entering the valley, Cortes's army marched past orderly fields of corn and spectacular flower gardens unlike anything to be seen in Spain. Indians lined the roads and viewed Cortes's battered veterans with awe. Some curiosity seekers (or spies sent by Montezuma) stole into the Spaniards' camp at night, only to be killed by alert sentries. Chiefs from the valley's towns greeted Cortes, often taking him out of earshot of the Aztec ambassadors and begging him to save them from Montezuma's oppression. The captain-general told each local leader that he had come to bring justice to the land and would help the people when the time was right. The chiefs also warned Cortes not to enter Tenochtitlan, because Montezuma intended to trap and destroy the Spaniards. Always, Cortes cheerfully boasted that neither the Aztecs nor any other nation could destroy his army.

Cortes in Tenochtitlan

As the Spaniards neared the Mexican capital, Montezuma increasingly believed that Cortes was invincible. Runners steadily brought him news of Spanish military and diplomatic successes. Nothing seemed to stop the European invaders. One last group of ambassadors sent by Montezuma, armed with bribes and promises of loyalty to Charles, had begged Cortes to return to Spain. The result of their mission, however, had been to convince the captain-general that the riches of Tenochtitlan exceeded his highest expectation. Each step closer to the gleaming white city on the lake filled the conquistadors with greater anticipation—and the lord of the Aztecs with greater dread.

At dawn on November 8, 1519, the army marched into Tenochtitlan. The cavalry under Cortes led the way, the horses' steel-shod hooves clattering on the stone causeway that connected the city with the lakeshore. Close behind followed the

Accompanied by Tlaxcalan allies, Cortes and his cavalry march across the causeway leading into Tenochtitlan.

Spanish infantry, tough veterans in battered armor, marching just ahead of six thousand copper-skinned Tlaxcalans. Thousands of Aztecs glided along the lake in canoes and gazed at this army from two worlds.

After marching across the causeway, a distance of nearly two miles, the conquistadors passed through a fortress gate. There they met several hundred Aztec nobles who greeted them and announced Montezuma's approach. After an hour of Indian ritual, the Spanish army crossed a heavy wooden drawbridge and entered the city's gate. Sitting astride his charger, Cortes saw hundreds of Aztec nobles in gaudy feathered robes approaching in solemn procession. In the midst of the nobles marched four brawny men of high rank. With downcast eyes and measured

Once inside the city, Cortes is met by a procession of elaborately dressed noblemen and the great king Montezuma transported on a golden chair.

step they carried a golden litter [sedan chair] bearing the great king, Montezuma.

Cortes leapt down from his horse, casting his reins to a page, and approached the king. Montezuma descended from the litter, stepping on cotton cloth spread to keep his royal feet from touching the ground. A nobleman held each of the king's arms to ease his way. Brilliant green feather robes decorated with pearls covered Montezuma, and from his head to the soles of his sandals the sun reflected on glittering gold. Cortes extended his arms to embrace the Aztec monarch, but the Aztec nobles blocked his path, shocked that anyone would attempt to touch the sacred personage.

Undaunted, Cortes hung a necklace of cut glass and pearls around the king's neck. To sixteenth-century Europeans such baubles were inexpensive trade goods. To the Aztecs, who lacked the skills to produce glass, the beads were priceless. Not to be outdone, Montezuma placed two skillfully carved gold necklaces around Cortes's neck. The Aztec nobles marveled that their great king had actually touched the visitor, an act normally considered beneath the monarch's dignity.

Montezuma and Cortes meet and exchange necklaces. Aztec nobles were shocked that their king actually touched the visitor, an act they considered beneath his dignity.

After the Aztec nobles had formally greeted Cortes, Montezuma ordered the Spanish soldiers taken to one of the city's many palaces and promised to visit them later. As his men ate and rested, Cortes considered the building's defensive possibilities. After all, the Spaniards were now deep inside the capital of a people that terrorized a vast domain. The conquistadors placed cannon at key entry points, posted guards, and began to convert their lodgings into a fortress. It was a good decision.

As promised, Montezuma returned. Seating himself on a throne prepared for the occasion, he apologized for having tried to keep the Spaniards out of Tenochtitlan. Some of his nobles, he explained, feared the Spaniards. Now it was obvious that Cortes posed no threat to the Aztecs, the king continued. Montezuma also made it clear that he considered Cortes the fulfillment of his ancestors' prophecy—the white-skinned one from the land where the sun rises:

> We have always . . . believed that some day men would come from those parts to . . . rule us, and I think you are the

ones, for judging by the direction you came from, and what you tell of the great King . . . who sent you, you knew of us. And so, my lord captain, you may be sure that we shall obey you, if you are not . . . tricking us, and that we shall share what we have with you.[19]

Cortes told Montezuma just enough truth. He and his men did indeed come from the land where the sun rises.

Protected for the moment by his reputation as the eastern ruler of Aztec legend, Cortes persuaded Montezuma to take a group of Spanish officers on a tour of Tenochtitlan. More than idle curiosity motivated the captain-general. If his command was to survive in this vast, potentially hostile city, he needed to make plans, and to make plans he had to scout his surroundings. No place provided a better vantage point than the great temple that dominated the city's skyline.

Montezuma seemed happy to show his city to the Spaniards. The astonished conquistadors walked down stone streets passing between orderly whitewashed stone buildings. Here and there giant murals adorned walls. Canoes flitted about on canals that served as streets much as they did in Venice, Italy. The Spaniards passed through a marketplace where robes, cloth, hides, food, slaves, jewelry, and gold were sold in seemingly limitless supply. In the great square, at least forty thousand merchants and buyers haggled over the bounty of the Aztecs.

Montezuma Greets Cortes

Hieroglyphics of Aztec documents indicate that Montezuma initially appeared to believe that Cortes had been sent by the white god of popular legend. Cortes did nothing to change the ruler's mind. This excerpt from General History of the Things of New Spain *gives Sahagun's translation of the Aztecs' report of the first meeting of the two leaders.*

"[Montezuma] said to [Cortes]: 'O our lord, thou hast suffered fatigue, thou hast endured weariness. Thou hast come to arrive on earth. Thou hast come to govern thy city of Mexico [Tenochtitlan]; thou hast come to descend upon thy . . . seat [throne] which for a moment I have . . . guarded for thee. . . . I have gazed at the unknown place whence thou has come—from among the clouds. . . . And now it hath been fulfilled; thou hast come. . . . Peace be with thee. Rest thyself. Visit thy palace. . . .'

And when [Cortes] had heard Moctezuma's words, he [said] . . . 'Let Moctezuma put his heart at ease; let him not be frightened. We love him much. Now our hearts are indeed satisfied, for we know him, we hear him. For a long time we have wished to see him, to look upon his face. And this we have seen.'"

The Great Temple

Above all stood the temple, perhaps three hundred feet square at the base and over a hundred feet high. Montezuma had preceded the Spaniards to the summit, to prepare the priests and the gods for visitors. Accustomed to making the long, difficult climb supported by two nobles, the king instructed two priests to assist Cortes so he would not suffer fatigue. The captain-general refused their help and climbed the 114 steps unaided. At the summit, Montezuma greeted him and commented that surely the effort must have tired him. Cortes dismissed the thought. Nothing ever tired the Spaniards, he assured Montezuma.

Cortes surveyed the city. With over sixty thousand buildings, Tenochtitlan eas-

(Above) Aztecs traverse the island in canoes on one of the many canals that crisscrossed Tenochtitlan. (Left) The surrounding wall and entrance to the Great Temple, the ceremonial building upon which the Aztecs practiced human sacrifice.

ily held ten times the population of any city in Spain. Clear water gushed from fountains supplied by stone aqueducts stretching to the hills. Far beneath him, Cortes saw the causeways joined by drawbridges crossing the lake. The bridges, which provided the only access to Tenochtitlan, could be raised to keep out intruders—or to keep them in. Near the temple stood a barracks housing ten thousand warriors. Around the barracks rose a stone wall surrounded by the sculpted image of a feathered and fanged serpent—the god Quetzalcoatl in one of his more intimidating forms.

The lord of the Aztecs led the little band of Spaniards into a sanctuary atop the temple. Two large, grinning idols stood in the room, decorated with gems and golden objects shaped like hearts. Smoke from burning incense curled from braziers, and in the dim light the Spaniards could see three human hearts smoldering in the metal pans. The smell of death hung heavily in the room, revolting even the battle-hardened Spanish soldiers. Bernal Diaz was horror-struck:

> All the walls of the oratory [temple sanctuary] were so splashed with blood that they were black, the floor was the same and the whole place stank vilely. . . .
>
> The walls were so clotted with blood and the soil so bathed with it that in the slaughter houses of Spain there is

Vigilant Precautions

Warned that Montezuma might attack his army, Cortes turned his quarters in Tenochtitlan into a fortress. In Conquest of Mexico, *historian William Prescott describes these preparations and the means Cortes used to intimidate the Aztecs.*

"The general [Cortes] . . . took . . . vigilant precautions for security, as if he had anticipated a siege. . . . He planted his cannon . . . to command the approaches, stationed his sentinels, . . . and . . . enforced . . . strict military discipline. . . . He well knew the importance to his little band . . . of conciliating the good will of the citizens; and . . . prohibited any soldier from leaving his quarters without orders, under pain of death. . . .

That evening the Spaniards celebrated their arrival in the Mexican capital by a general discharge of artillery. The thunder . . . filled the hearts of the superstitious Aztecs with dismay. It proclaimed to them that their city held . . . those dread beings . . . who could call down the thunderbolts to consume their enemies! It was doubtless the policy of Cortes . . . to impress the natives . . . with . . . awe of the supernatural powers of the Spaniards."

not such another stench. . . . We could hardly wait a moment to get out of it.[20]

Following Montezuma out of the temple sanctuary, the Spaniards gratefully drank in the fresh air. As calmly as possible, Cortes turned to the king and said he was amazed that so great a ruler would worship beings who were clearly not gods but different forms of the devil. Cortes then suggested that a cross be set up on the temple.

Outraged at the insult to Aztec gods, Montezuma told Cortes that his party must leave to permit the priests to offer sacrifices to atone for the Spaniards' blasphemy. The white men could erect an altar in front of their quarters, but no symbol of their religion would be permitted on the temple. Cortes decided not to press the issue and led his men back to the palace Montezuma had assigned them.

When the Spanish carpenters were building the altar, they noticed a freshly plastered area on a wall. On Cortes's orders, the carpenters removed the plaster and found a secret room filled with gold, silver, and gems. They had stumbled across the treasure Montezuma's father had left him—the tribute of hundreds of Indian towns. Cortes coolly told his men to say nothing of the wealth and ordered the room resealed.

Cortes Arrests Montezuma

After a week in Tenochtitlan, the Spaniards had made little progress toward taking control of the city. Although they were treated as honored guests, they heard constant rumors from their Tlaxcalan allies of Aztec plots against the Europeans. More than once Cortes received false reports that the bridges had been raised to trap his men in the city.

Some of Cortes's officers urged him to return to Villa Rica as quickly as possible, but he dismissed the idea as impractical. They would be no safer, he argued, on the roads in the Aztec domain than in the city. Even if the army reached Villa Rica, it would have left Mexico unconquered, which not only would anger King Charles but would allow someone else to claim the land and its spoils. The officers suggested a bolder course—take Montezuma hostage. Diaz wrote that at first Cortes resisted the advice:

Cortes used cunning and manipulation to gain the upper hand over Montezuma, a feat many would have considered impossible.

Montezuma is taken captive and brought before Cortes. The king reluctantly surrendered after Cortes's soldiers threatened to take his life.

> When Cortes heard this he replied: "Don't you imagine, gentlemen, that I . . . am free from the same anxiety, you must have felt . . . but what possibility is there of our doing a deed of such great daring as to seize such a great prince in his own palace, surrounded . . . by his own guards and warriors . . . ?" Our Captains replied . . . that with smooth speeches he should be got out of his halls and brought to our quarters . . . and if he made a disturbance . . . that he would pay for it with his life; that if Cortes did not want to do this at once, he should give them permission . . . for they were ready for the work.[21]

Cortes agreed to the plan, and circumstances soon provided a pretext for making the arrest. Messengers brought word that on Montezuma's orders, Indians had killed one Spaniard and wounded six others at a town called Almeria. Cortes set the plan in motion. By threes and fours Spanish officers casually arrived at Montezuma's palace. Montezuma would not be alarmed, because he was used to the Spanish visitors and knew they carried their weapons everywhere. Cortes arrived last and suddenly accused the Aztec king of ordering the attack at Almeria.

Montezuma turned pale with terror and denied any involvement in the incident. Smoothly, Cortes accepted his explanation but added that Quauhpopoca, the leader of the attack, and all those who had conspired or participated in the action, would have to be punished. Montezuma quickly agreed and commanded some of his nobles to bring Quauhpopoca to Tenochtitlan.

Cortes assured Montezuma that he believed the king's claims of innocence but warned that Charles of Spain would require more proof. He ordered Montezuma to come with the Spaniards to their quarters until the matter was resolved. Determined not to be taken prisoner in his own kingdom, Montezuma resisted with lengthy arguments. After nearly two hours of debate, one of the Spanish officers lost patience and shouted angrily that Cortes should have Montezuma killed and be done with it. Surrounded by grim-faced Spaniards, each with one hand on his sword hilt, Montezuma agreed to go.

"The Most Beautiful Sight in the World"

When Cortes arrived in Mexico, Tenochtitlan was one of the largest cities on earth. In this excerpt from Cortes, *Gomara gives an impression of the city before the conquest.*

"Mexico was a city of sixty-thousand houses. . . . The main part of the city was surrounded by water. Its thoroughfares were of three kinds . . . one of water alone, with a great many bridges; others of earth alone; the third kind was of earth and water, where canoes could circulate. . . . Drinking water was brought in from a spring in the hill of Chapultepec. . . . Mexico-Tenochtitlan . . . can be approached by only three causeways. . . . The lake upon which Mexico is situated . . . is really two, . . . one saline [salty], bitter, and stinking, . . . the other of sweet water. . . . Upon these lakes float some two hundred thousand small boats. . . .

Mexico had many temples with towers, surmounted by chapels and altars, where the idols . . . were kept. . . . [The great temple] resembled a pyramid of Egypt, save that it [ended] in a square platform. . . . From it one had a fine view of the city and the lake with all its towns, the most beautiful sight in the world."

A reconstruction of the Great Temple and surrounding precinct. Cortes described the view from the top of the temple as "the most beautiful sight in the world."

Twenty days later, the Aztec nobles returned with Quauhpopoca, who was tried by a Spanish court and condemned to death. As the soldiers prepared to burn the chieftain at the stake, Cortes entered Montezuma's room and ordered him shackled. Frightened and surprised at the insult to his royal person, Montezuma roared angrily as he was placed in chains.

Cortes ordered spears, bows, arrows, and other wooden weapons taken from Tenochtitlan's arsenal to fuel the execution fire. In a square surrounded by armed Spanish soldiers, the people of Tenochtitlan silently watched a great Aztec noble die a fiery death. Quauhpopoca did not cry out. Cortes had Montezuma's chains removed after the execution, and the mightiest ruler in North America expressed thanks for this kindness.

In captivity, Montezuma became a pawn for the power-hungry Cortes. Upon his captor's command, Montezuma ordered his lords to pledge their loyalty to Cortes and King Charles of Spain.

The Captive King

Cortes and his men treated Montezuma respectfully and developed a friendly relationship with him. Occasionally, Montezuma and Cortes gambled for gold and gems. When the lord of the Aztecs caught the golden-haired Alvarado cheating on his master's behalf, he took it good-naturedly. Montezuma often gave his winnings to his favorites among the Spaniards, many of whom now wore their personal wealth in heavy gold chains around their necks.

Montezuma seemed anxious to cooperate with the Spaniards. He supplied Aztec carpenters to help Cortes's men build brigantines on the lake. Realizing how easily the Aztecs could trap his army in the city, the captain-general saw the ships as one more means of escape in an emergency. When the ships were completed, Cortes took his royal captive on excursions across the lake.

Many of the captain-general's actions served dual purposes. Montezuma's leisurely cruises gave the Spaniards opportunities to test their new vessels. Often, too, Cortes manipulated Montezuma emotionally. On several occasions, Cortes offered to permit Montezuma to return to his own palace, but the king refused, saying that his presence in the Spanish quarters protected the conquistadors from the wrath of the people. It is just as likely that Montezuma feared his own subjects might kill him for

Cortes Decides to Capture Montezuma

Although it appeared that Montezuma was arrested for having ordered an attack on the Spaniards near the coast, Cortes had additional motives. In this passage from his second letter to King Charles, he elaborates.

"I decided from what I had seen that it would benefit Your Royal service and our safety if Mutezuma were in my power . . . in order that he should not retreat from the willingness he showed to serve your Majesty . . . [and] obliterate [wipe out] all memory of us. . . .

Thinking of all the ways . . . to capture him without causing a disturbance, I remembered what the captain I had left in [Villa Rica de la] Vera Cruz had written me about . . . [the attack on the Spanish soldiers]. . . . I . . . went to Mutezuma's houses . . . and after having joked and exchanged pleasantries with him . . . I told him that I knew of . . . the Spaniards who had been killed . . . and that . . . Qualpopoca [Quauhpopoca] excused himself by saying that all had been done by Mutezuma's command. . . .

I . . . asked that he should stay in my quarters until the truth were known and he was shown to be blameless."

An embroidered cloth depicts the seizure of Montezuma. Cortes concocted a deceptive plan to accomplish the capture.

allowing the intruders to take him hostage. Cortes probably never intended to release his hostage and surely would have revoked the offer if the king had accepted it.

Clearly, the time had come to dispense with the pretense that Montezuma held unquestioned authority over the Aztec realms. At the captain-general's command, the Aztec king summoned his lords and ordered them to give their loyalty to Malinche—as the Aztecs of Tenochtitlan, like the Indians of the Yucatan region, called Cortes—and to Charles of Spain, Malinche's king.

In his biography of Cortes, Gomara wrote that Montezuma reminded the Aztec nobles that the kingdom was not his own to keep: "The king whom we have been expecting for so many years is the one who has sent these Spaniards. . . . You will please me by giving yourselves to this captain . . . to whom I have already submitted."[22] One by one the weeping nobles swore their loyalty to Cortes and Charles. The prophecy was fulfilled.

With the Aztec lords in a submissive mood, Cortes reminded Montezuma of the Spanish king's desire for tribute. Montezuma willingly surrendered the roomful of treasure the Spanish had discovered earlier. Apologizing for its small size, the Aztec king ordered his people to bring more gold and silver from existing mines and to help the Spaniards open new ones.

Cortes had wanted to keep the treasure in one place, but the men, believing that Cortes and his officers had already taken much for themselves, demanded their share. Unable to persuade the soldiers to wait, Cortes ordered some of the treasure distributed. The common soldiers, complaining that they had been led to expect a larger share of the booty, refused to accept the pittance they were offered; they understood that Cortes remained in control of most of the treasure. Under Spanish supervision, Indian artisans converted the gold and silver into more portable forms, changing priceless statuary and jewelry into ingots and chains.

While the booty was being prepared for shipment, Montezuma warned Cortes that Huitzilopochtli had instructed the Aztec priests to destroy the Spaniards. Earnestly, Montezuma urged Cortes and his men to return to Spain for their own safety. Cortes promised him they would gladly leave as soon as his ships had been rebuilt, and the Aztec emperor sent Indian workers to help the Spanish shipwrights at Villa Rica.

Cortes had other plans. Stalling for time, he secretly instructed his men to work as slowly as possible while he sought reinforcements from Hispaniola. As the construction continued, Montezuma sent word to Cortes that he urgently wished to see him. Warned by Marina that Montezuma might be planning an ambush, Cortes told his men to prepare for the worst.

Narvaez

In good spirits when Cortes arrived, Montezuma announced that more Spanish ships had arrived at Villa Rica, and therefore Cortes could leave for Spain immediately. According to Diaz, the captain-general wisely concealed his true feelings at the news:

> When Cortes heard about the ships . . . he rejoiced greatly and said:

Rendering Montezuma Contemptible

Writing from a nineteenth-century point of view, historian William Prescott, in his Conquest of Mexico, *defends Cortes's decisions to burn Quauhpopoca at the stake and take Montezuma hostage.*

"[The conquistadors'] standard of right and wrong, in reference to the natives, was a very simple one. Despising them as an outlawed race, without God in the world, they . . . held it to be their 'mission' . . . to conquer and convert. . . . By the execution . . . they struck terror not only into the capital, but throughout the country. It proclaimed that not a hair of a Spaniard was to be touched [without punishment]! By rendering Montezuma contemptible [deserving scorn] in his own eyes and those of his subjects, Cortes deprived him of the support of his people, and forced him to lean on the arm of a stranger. It was a politic [wise] proceeding—to which few men could have been equal, who had a touch of humanity in their natures."

"Thank God! who at the right moment provides for us. . . ." But Cortes was very thoughtful, for he well understood that that fleet was sent by Diego Velasquez the Governor of Cuba against him and all of us.[23]

Spanish messengers bringing reports from the coast soon confirmed his fears. Velasquez had sent Panfilo de Narvaez, a Spanish noble, to New Spain with eighteen ships and fourteen hundred men to capture and punish Cortes and his men. One of Narvaez's officers even bragged that he would cut off one of Cortes's ears, roast it, and eat it. To make matters worse, Narvaez had sent word to Montezuma that once he had captured Cortes, all the Spanish colonizers would leave New Spain.

Cortes acted boldly. Using some of the treasure he had collected, he sent bribes to certain of Narvaez's officers, along with promises of more to come if they joined him in the conquest of Mexico. Then, leaving Alvarado with a small force to hold the city, Cortes marched with 260 Spaniards and some Tlaxcalan allies to attack Narvaez.

Chapter

7 The Sorrowful Night

His troops heavily outnumbered, Cortes depended both on his veteran soldiers' experience and on psychological warfare. The captain-general sent letters to Narvaez, who had quartered his men in Cempoala. Pledging cooperation, he warned that fighting among the Spaniards might encourage the Indians to rebel. Along with the letters, Cortes sent still more bribes of gold and silver. These, and the gifts he had received from Montezuma, Narvaez unwisely hoarded for himself, causing complaints among his men, who felt entitled to a share.

The captain-general took care not to let it be known that the enemy's will to resist might be weakened by bribes and persuasion. Cortes realized that the strategy might fail, and he wanted his troops prepared to face fierce opposition. He sought every possible advantage. He sent some men from Villa Rica disguised as Indians to infiltrate Narvaez's camp. He had Indians make copper-tipped pikes (spears), which were longer than those the Spaniards commonly used, to arm his men. As always, he appealed to the soldiers' honor, promising that God would strengthen their hands in battle, and to their greed, reminding them of the wealth they would gain through victory.

In contrast, Narvaez scoffed at Cortes's peace overtures and boasted that he would win an easy victory. Any of his men who spoke well of Cortes were imprisoned. Otherwise, Narvaez and his troops passed the time in looting the Cempoalans and taking their women as mistresses. Accustomed to Cortes's rough justice, the Fat Cacique told Narvaez that the captain-general, who had never abused the Indians, would set things right when he returned. In his account of the

Cortes and a small force march out of Tenochtitlan to battle Narvaez's army. After having come this far, Cortes was determined to let nothing stop him from conquering Mexico.

conquest, Bernal Diaz quotes the Cempoalan chieftain's warning to Narvaez:

> What are you about? You are behaving very carelessly; do you think that Malinche and the Teules [gods] that he brings with him are the same as you are? Well, I tell you that when you least expect it he will be here and will kill you.[24]

Narvaez and his officers ridiculed the Fat Cacique for his superstitious awe of Cortes but prepared defenses against surprise attack.

The attack came just as predicted. Although European armies of that time rarely fought at night or in bad weather, Cortes did both, attacking the rival Spanish camp suddenly through darkness and rain. As Narvaez's men stumbled to their feet, bolts (crossbow arrows) whizzed through the air and the sound of gunfire shattered the jungle's silence. And on top of the initial surprise, the just-woken soldiers were to be misled by another one of Cortes's clever plans. Sixteenth-century Spaniards used matchlock muskets, which were fired by burning cords (matches); at night, the burning matches glowed in the dark and were easily visible. This potential disadvantage was turned in their favor. When Cortes's men advanced, thousands of fireflies rose around them. In the confusion, Narvaez's men mistook the fireflies for musket flashes and thought they were outnumbered.

Narvaez's cavalrymen leapt to their horses but immediately fell to the ground,

Psychological Warfare Against Narvaez

Narvaez sent a priest and some messengers to order Gonzalo de Sandoval, one of Cortes's lieutenants, to surrender Villa Rica. Sandoval sent them bound as captives to Cortes. In his chronicle, Diaz says that Cortes converted the captives to his cause.

"He sent out horses for the three principal persons and ordered them at once to be released . . . and wrote to them that he regretted that Sandoval should have treated them so disrespectfully. . . . When the priest and his companions saw how great a city was Mexico [Tenochtitlan] and the wealth of gold that we possessed, . . . and the frank open-heartedness of Cortes, they were amazed, and . . . Cortes . . . talked to them in such a way with promises and flattery and even by greasing their palms with little ingots and jewels of gold, that when he sent them back to their Narvaez . . . although they had set out as fierce as lions, they returned thoroughly tamed, and offered themselves to Cortes as his servants. . . . They began to persuade all the camp of Narvaez to come over to our side."

Cortes rallies his soldiers with promises of victory and fortune. The ranks of his army quickly swelled when Cortes gave Narvaez's men the option of aiding in the conquest or immediate death.

because Cortes had sent scouts to cut the leather straps that secured the saddles. As Narvaez desperately tried to rally his confused troops, a pike slashed through one eye. The stricken commander's screams rose above the sounds of battle, demoralizing his own men and inspiring Cortes's. Once the wounded Narvaez had been captured, his men became a leaderless rabble. Their determination weakened by bribes and fear, Narvaez's army began to surrender. It was over in minutes.

Faced with watching over a thousand prisoners, Cortes offered two options: be put to the sword on the spot or swear loyalty to Cortes and share in Mexico's rich spoils. Given the choices of wealth and glory or certain death, Narvaez's men quickly swore allegiance to Cortes. They were told that they would not regret the decision.

To prevent any of his new recruits from returning to Cuba, Cortes ordered Narvaez's ships disabled. Then, with an army more than tripled in strength, the captain-general led his troops back toward Tenochtitlan. During the march, a messenger from Alvarado arrived to announce that the people of Tenochtitlan had turned on the Spanish garrison and besieged it. Cortes ordered the pace quickened.

After days of forced marches, on June 24, 1520, the tired army passed through the gates of Tenochtitlan. No chiefs greeted them; the streets were deserted. Once inside the Spanish quarters, Cortes asked Alvarado what had happened.

Trapped in Tenochtitlan

Sheepishly, Alvarado explained that he had granted the Aztecs permission to celebrate the festival of Huitzilopochtli, but had become uneasy about his decision, fearing that because the garrison was reduced in strength, the Aztecs might choose this opportunity to seize the Spaniards for sacrificial victims. An impetuous and violent man, Alvarado had unleashed his cavalry on the Aztecs as they danced in the streets around the idol. With lance and sword, the riders had cut down hundreds of panic-stricken worshipers. Survivors had aroused the city, and an enraged multitude had armed themselves and driven the Spaniards back into their fortress.

Cortes's worst nightmare had happened. His command was trapped in the city. He scolded Alvarado for behaving like a madman and left to evaluate the situation. The Aztecs had burned his four brigantines and destroyed the causeway bridges. Alvarado had dug a well within the Spanish quarters to supply drinking water, but food was scarce. After inspecting the fortress's defenses, Cortes summoned an Aztec noble and commanded him to open the market so the Spaniards could obtain food. The noble left the captain-general's presence, but instead of making arrangements for the Spaniards to do their shopping, he incited the Aztecs to attack. Soon the streets overflowed with howling Aztec warriors, and Indians hurled stones from the rooftops onto any Spaniards who ventured into the open.

As hopeless as the situation looked, Cortes still held an advantage—his royal hostage, Montezuma. The captain-general led the king to a rooftop and commanded him to order his people to return peace-

Unusual Tactics

Cortes often surprised his enemies by unusual tactics. In this portion of his chronicle, quoted in The Conquistadors: First Person Accounts of Mexico, *translated by Patricia de Fuentes, Andres de Tapia describes Cortes's decision to attack Narvaez's camp on a rainy night.*

"It had been raining and we were wet, and eager to roast the deer and pigs the horsemen had killed, but when we pitched camp a league [roughly three miles] away from the enemy the marques [Cortes] ordered us not to make a fire so that we should not be seen. After posting a double watch we tried to rest but were unable to because we were wet and there was a cold wind. The marques awakened, or rather since he could not sleep he called without sounding the drum and said to us: 'Gentlemen, you know it is quite usual for the military man to say "attack the enemy at dawn"; so if we have been perceived, that is the hour they will expect us. And if they have not perceived us, in any event we cannot sleep and may as well use the time fighting and enjoying the benefit of our victory rather than waste it suffering in the cold. . . .'

When we responded that we would win or die he started the march."

Montezuma collapses from an attack by his own people. The fatal injury occurred as he was preparing to order an end to attacks on the Spaniards.

fully to their homes. Shielded by Cortes and his men, Montezuma faced the multitude, but before he could speak, some Aztecs cursed and stoned their captured leader. Montezuma was struck in the head and collapsed senseless. Spanish soldiers carried the wounded monarch inside the fortress, where the man who had been the mightiest ruler in North America died two days later, a captive in his own land.

The Sorrowful Night

A period of desperation followed. Each morning, Cortes led his soldiers and their Tlaxcalan allies in pitched battle to the causeways, where they filled the gaps with debris, to be able to cross the lake. In addition, they killed hundreds, perhaps thousands, of Aztecs. But each day reinforcements replenished the Indians' ranks, and at night, workers reopened the gaps in the causeways. The Aztecs no longer seemed intimidated by the bearded men. Wounded and terrified, Cortes's troops begged him to take them out of the city before they were all killed. Cortes later wrote King Charles of his decision to evacuate the fortress in Tenochtitlan:

> Because I had seen the great danger we were in and the great harm which the Indians did us every day, . . . and because all of my company, the greater part of whom were so badly wounded they could no longer fight, had often entreated me to depart, I determined to leave that same night.[25]

At Cortes's command, the Spanish soldiers constructed a portable wooden bridge, which they planned to move from gap to gap as they made their escape. When darkness had fallen, as the Spaniards prepared to leave, Cortes ordered King Charles's share of the treasure to be loaded onto several horses. The rest of the treasure he offered to the men, warning them not to carry too much, since they would need to travel quickly. While Cortes's veterans followed his advice and took only small amounts of gold, Narvaez's men took all they could carry. Greed would cost them their lives.

On June 30, 1520, Cortes, his Spaniards, and their Indian allies stole into the night as the Aztecs lay sleeping about the city. Using their portable bridge, the little army crossed the first gap safely, but then the bridge became too deeply embedded in the muck to be moved. As the Spaniards struggled to free the bridge, Aztec sentries awakened the city, and warriors swarmed the causeway. Panic-stricken soldiers threw themselves into the water, desperately trying to cross the gap. Those heavily burdened by gold sank to their death, forming a bridge of human bodies to the other side.

Forcing his mount to swim the last gaps, Cortes reached the mainland and looked back on his ruined command. Most of his Indian allies and all but four hundred out of fourteen hundred of his soldiers were dead. All the survivors were wounded and exhausted. His men had saved a few of their crossbows, but all the cannon, muskets, and powder were lost. Nearly all the treasure lay at the bottom of the lake, mingled with the bodies of many soldiers. Behind him stood a victorious

Spanish soldiers plunge to their deaths during the "sorrowful night." The battle was devastating to the Spaniards, who lost thousands of lives and most of the priceless treasures that they had acquired.

Cortes Cheats Death

The Spaniards called their retreat from Tenochtitlan the Noche Triste, or sorrowful night. In the Conquest of Mexico, *William Prescott describes the chaos that surrounded Cortes as he fought for his life during the retreat.*

"The infantry followed pellmell, heaped . . . on one another, frequently pierced by shafts or struck down by the war-clubs of the Aztecs; while many an unfortunate victim was dragged half-stunned on board their canoes, to be reserved for a . . . more dreadful death. . . .

The opening in the causeway, meanwhile, was filled up with the wreck of . . . ammunition-wagons, heavy guns, bales of rich stuffs scattered over the waters, chests of solid ingots, and bodies of men and horses, till over this dismal ruin a passage was gradually formed. . . . Cortes . . . found a place that was fordable [could be crossed], where halting with the water up to his saddle-girths, he endeavoured to check the confusion, and lead his followers by a safer path to the opposite bank. But his voice was lost in the wild uproar, and finally, hurrying on with the tide, he pressed forwards with a few trusty cavaliers. . . . Those fared best, as the general had predicted, who travelled lightest; and many were the unfortunate wretches, who, weighed down by the fatal gold which they loved so well, were buried with it in the salt floods of the lake."

Aztec army, and ahead lay the cities of the Aztecs' subjects. Gomara tells of the despair Cortes felt that night:

> Cortes stopped and even sat down, not to rest, but to mourn over the dead and those still living, and to consider the heavy blow that fate had dealt him in the loss of so many friends, such treasures, such authority, and such a great city and kingdom . . . because all his men were wounded and he knew not what way to turn. . . . Who . . . would not weep at the death and ruin of those who had entered in such triumph, pomp, and rejoicing? In the rout of this sad night . . . 450 Spaniards died, 4,000 Indian friends, 46 horses, and I believe, all the prisoners [Aztec nobles and Montezuma's children]. Some say more, some less, but this is the truest number. [26]

With the shrieks of his dying comrades drifting across the lake, the captain-general leaned against a cypress tree and wept.

Chapter

8 The Return to Tenochtitlan

Cortes had little time to mourn. He led his exhausted men past the lakeshore city of Tacuba to an open plain, where they drove away a few Indians and climbed to the summit of a temple they could defend. All through the day and into the night, Spanish sentries held the Aztec skirmishers at bay while their comrades slept fitfully. Near midnight, after Cortes's men had rested and dressed their wounds, they built many campfires to deceive the enemy and quietly slipped away.

If any hope remained for Cortes and his men, it lay in Tlaxcala. Despite their initial resistance, the Tlaxcalans had proven faithful allies and steadfast in their hatred of the Aztecs. If the Spaniards could reach the Tlaxcalan republic, they might find refuge. Many Spaniards, suspecting that Tlaxcalan friendship depended on the Europeans' ability to destroy the hated Aztecs, feared that the Indian allies might decide it would be safer to join their old enemies.

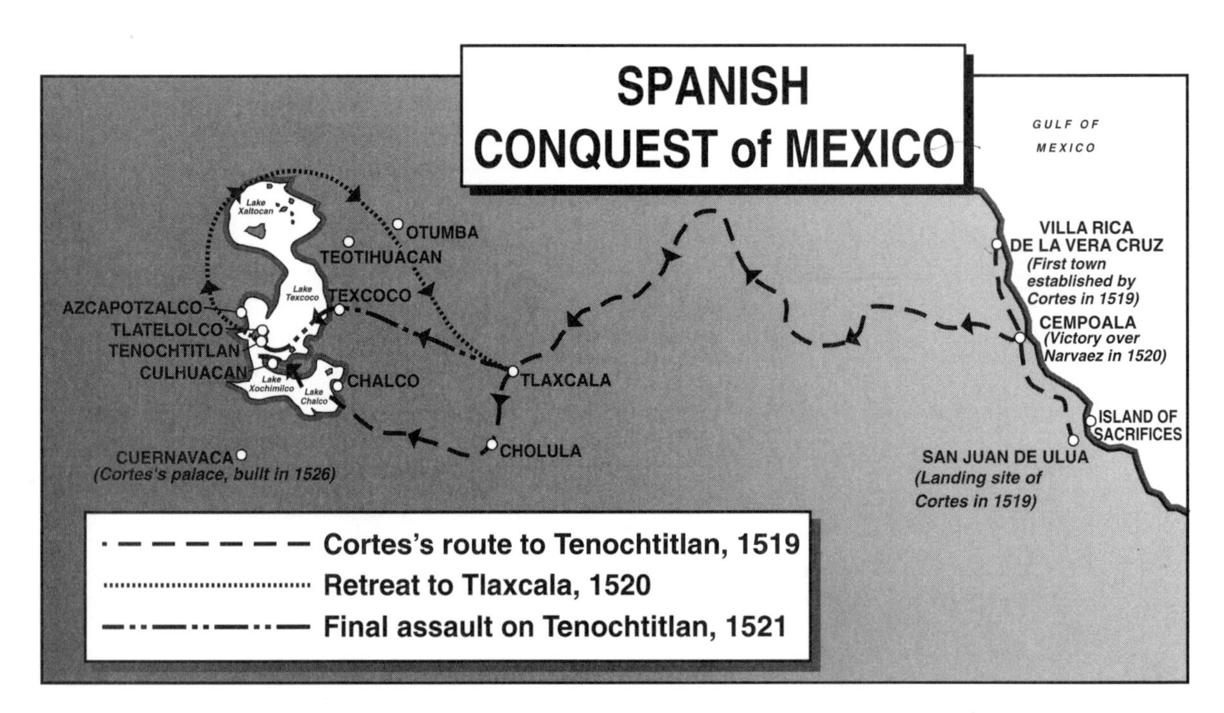

Ignoring these uncertainties, Cortes led his men toward the mountains. As disastrous as the "sorrowful night" had been, hope remained. Both Marina and Aguilar had survived the retreat. Remarkably, all Cortes's most trusted commanders had also fought their way to safety—the amazing Pedro de Alvarado escaped pursuing Aztecs by pole vaulting with a lance across the last gap. And although the Aztecs still followed the Spaniards, they seemed content not to force a full-blown battle.

For eight days the battered army pressed on. By July 7, 1520, the Aztec hordes had slackened their attacks and merely hovered near the army's line of march, shouting insults and threats. Cortes and his men passed by the massive temples of the sun and the moon, which had stood since ancient times in a valley the Indians called the "Path of Death." Over the next mountain and across the next plain lay Tlaxcala.

Cortes valiantly fends off Aztec attackers during the Battle of Otumba. With skill and bravery, the captain-general led his army to victory.

Battle of Otumba

On the morning of July 8, Cortes led his army into the Valley of Otumba. There two hundred thousand Aztec warriors in their white quilted cotton armor covered the valley like drifted snow. Aztec nobles in bright feathered robes, carrying golden shields, added splashes of color to the Indian legions. The vast host, confident, patient, and determined, blocked the path to Tlaxcala.

Retreat was impossible. Cortes's army had stayed just ahead of a pursuing Aztec force for days. There was no escape. Facing an army much larger than his own, his men weakened by disease and fatigue and armed only with swords and lances, Cortes decided to attack.

The little army plunged into the midst of the Aztec horde and was soon surrounded by Indian warriors. Following Cortes's orders, the Spaniards singled out enemy chieftains, hoping to spread confusion by killing the leaders. For hours, the Spanish soldiers and their Tlaxcalan allies fought desperately, knowing that defeat meant death on the battlefield or sacrifice on the Aztec altars. Cortes rode one horse to exhaustion and mounted another, fighting madly and looking for an opportunity to save his command. Just as it seemed the Spaniards would be overwhelmed, he saw his chance.

Atop a small rise in the distance, in a litter carried by Indian nobles, sat an Aztec chieftain named Cihuaca. Seeing by his robes and golden banner that Cihuaca

Otumba

Drawing on Aztec accounts, Bernardino de Sahagun provided his own narrative of events of the conquest. In this excerpt from General History of the Things of New Spain, *he describes Cortes's critical leadership at the Battle of Otumba.*

"The Mexicans . . . came with great force, eager to overwhelm [the Spaniards]. . . . Being thus hemmed in on all sides, the Spaniards started to strike at them, killing [the Mexicans] like flies. No sooner were they slain than they were replaced with fresh ones. The Spaniards were like an islet in the sea, beaten by the waves on all sides. . . .

When it came noon . . . the Spaniards began to lag. Seeing this, Captain . . . Cortes . . . bravely encouraged his men, saying . . . 'Oh my brothers, what are you doing? Why don't you exert yourselves? Why lose heart and allow yourselves to be slaughtered like pigs by those cursed idolaters?'

He said these words in a very loud and sad voice. From atop his horse . . . he . . . saw . . . the commander of the Mexicans. . . . Then [Cortes] summoned his horsemen. . . . [They] burst into the enemy camp. . . . Once there they lanced the commander . . . putting the rest to flight. . . . The Spaniards were left victorious while all their enemies rapidly disappeared."

Amidst a field strewn with bodies of dead Aztec warriors, Cortes proclaims victory at Otumba.

Tlaxcalan allies gather supplies and help the Spaniards build new brigantines in preparation for a renewed attack on Tenochtitlan.

commanded the Aztecs, Cortes, followed by four of his horsemen, charged through the warriors, killed the chieftain, and held aloft his banner. In an instant, the confused Aztec warriors fled the field, leaving Cortes victorious. In his history of the conquest, William Prescott praises Cortes's courage and good fortune: "The star of Cortes was in the ascendant. Had it been otherwise, not a Spaniard would have survived that day to tell the bloody tale of the battle of Otumba."[27]

After the Battle of Otumba, the Tlaxcalans welcomed the Spaniards into their republic. Several of Cortes's men begged him to rest the army in the safety of Tlaxcala and then to return to Villa Rica, where they could rebuild the ships and escape to Cuba. By now they should have known their commander better. The captain-general was already planning the army's return to Tenochtitlan.

Within three weeks of arriving in Tlaxcala, Cortes raided towns that had fought the Spaniards during the retreat from Tenochtitlan. In each town, the Spaniards took Indians as slaves, branding them on the cheek and setting aside allotments for King Charles and Cortes. Many of the common soldiers grumbled that the captain-general took the most attractive female slaves for himself. Cortes also collected the treasure that had been saved during the retreat, outfitted a ship, and sent some of his men to purchase military supplies in Spain.

For months, men and equipment trickled into Villa Rica. Velasquez, thinking Narvaez now controlled New Spain, sent ships bearing supplies and reinforcements, all of which Cortes immediately seized. More and more Spanish vessels visited Villa Rica. Each of these Cortes also recruited or purchased until he had acquired a number of cannon and commanded over nine hundred well-equipped soldiers.

Anxious to avenge the deaths of their kinsmen, the Tlaxcalans threw themselves into Cortes's preparations. Thousands of Indian allies helped the Spaniards build new brigantines, which the Spaniards would use to take control of the lakes around Tenochtitlan. Others gathered supplies to sustain a large army in the field for a long campaign.

As usual, while Cortes prepared for war he offered peace. He sent some prisoners of war with a message to Montezuma's successor, Cuauhtemoc, saying that the Spaniards would not go to war if the Mexicans would only disarm themselves. Otherwise, Cortes would destroy Tenochtitlan and its people. Young and determined, the new Aztec ruler sent no reply. Like Cortes, Cuauhtemoc was preparing his people for war.

Cortes assembled his men for the march back to Tenochtitlan in December 1520. The new army dwarfed the force he had commanded in 1519. Chiefs from all over the region, convinced that Malinche would triumph over the Aztecs, offered Cortes their loyalty. During the campaign he sometimes commanded as many as two hundred thousand Indian allies.

Montezuma's successor, Cuauhtemoc (pictured), was determined to defend his city at any cost. He began preparing his people for the Spaniards' return.

Siege of Tenochtitlan

Beginning in late December 1520, Cortes took control of cities that lay in the Valley of Mexico. Some cities, driven by fear, joined Cortes when the army returned to the valley. Others resisted and fell to the conquistadors. By May 1521, Cortes's army had surrounded Tenochtitlan and demolished the great aqueducts that carried the city's water supply. Thousands of Tlaxcalans carried the brigantines to the lake, where the warships swept the Aztecs' canoes from the waters. Now the capital's teeming multitudes had to survive on water from a few shallow wells and the food in their storehouses. Cortes had made time his ally.

In addition, an invisible Spanish ally had entered the city: The Aztecs had no immunity against smallpox, but one of Narvaez's men had carried the disease into Tenochtitlan. Although his people faced plague and starvation, Cuauhtemoc vowed to fight to the death.

For months Cortes sent his forces into battle across the causeways, burning build-

Cortes Intimidates Conspirators

During the siege of Tenochtitlan, Cortes learned of a plot to murder him, engineered by some of the men who had originally been with Narvaez. In The Discovery and Conquest of Mexico, *Diaz describes how Cortes, unable to spare any soldiers, found a way to punish the ringleaders and intimidate the other conspirators into obedience.*

"We . . . went with Cortes to the lodging of Antonio de Villafana [the conspiracy's leader] and . . . laid hands on [him] and the Captains and soldiers who were with him. . . . As soon as we held Villafana prisoner Cortes drew from his [Villafana's] breast [pocket] the memorandum . . . with the signatures of all who were in the conspiracy, and after he had read it and had seen that there were many persons of quality in it, so as not to dishonour them, he spread the report that Villafana had swallowed the memorandum and that he [Cortes] had neither seen nor read it, and at once brought him to trial. . . . After Villafana had confessed with the priest . . . they hanged him from the window of the room where he lodged. . . .

Cortes did not wish that anyone else should be dishonoured in that affair, although at that time many were made prisoners . . . to frighten them. . . . Although from that time forth he showed great kindness to those who were in the conspiracy, he distrusted them."

ings along the shore, filling gaps where bridges had been removed, and clearing Aztec fortifications. Each night after Cortes had withdrawn his men, the Aztecs reopened the gaps and rebuilt their fortifications.

Cortes soon realized that the Aztecs had improved their fighting techniques. For example, the Indians used long spears tipped with captured Spanish swords to kill horses before the cavalrymen could get close enough to strike with their own weapons. More than once, the Aztecs cleverly retreated and drew the conquistadors into ambushes. On one fatal day, the overconfident conquistadors, anxious to capture Tenochtitlan's central plaza, advanced too quickly and, ignoring Cortes's orders, failed to fill causeway gaps behind them. The Aztecs counterattacked and killed forty Spaniards and many Indian allies; they carried away Spanish captives for sacrifice, and nearly captured Cortes. In his third letter to King Charles, Cortes described the disaster:

> I saw the Spaniards and many of our allies in full retreat with the enemy like hounds at their heels; and . . . I began to cry "Stop! Stop . . . !" As . . . I saw that my men were being killed, I determined to make a stand and die fighting.[28]

The Decision to Destroy Tenochtitlan

During the siege of Tenochtitlan, Cortes saw himself as putting down a rebellion against Spanish rule. In this excerpt from his third letter to King Charles, Cortes expresses amazement at the Aztecs' willingness to fight in the face of certain defeat.

"When I saw how rebellious the people of this city were, and how they seemed more determined to perish . . . I did not know by what means we might relieve ourselves of all these dangers and hardships, and yet avoid destroying them and their city which was indeed the most beautiful thing in the world. . . . They paid no heed to us when we told them . . . there was no one in all the land to help them, nor could they acquire maize or meat or fruit or water. . . . The more such things were told them, the less signs they showed of weakening; rather they seemed to attack each time with greater spirit. Then, seeing . . . that we had been besieging the city for more than forty-five days, I decided . . . to . . . raze [demolish] all the houses on both sides of the streets . . . so that we should move not a step without leaving everything behind us in ruins; and all the canals were to be filled in, no matter how long it took us."

Cortes's forces battle the brave Aztecs atop the Great Temple of Tenochtitlan.

Cortes narrowly escaped death. That night the temples of Tenochtitlan glowed red with the light of torches and braziers. The drum of Huitzilopochtli throbbed steadily, and the wail of conch horns echoed throughout the valley. Cortes and his men watched across the lake as Aztec priests carried their captured comrades to the temple summit to be sacrificed. There was nothing they could do to help their friends.

The Aztec victory was short-lived. Cortes, his offers of peace rejected and no end to the siege in sight, decided to destroy Tenochtitlan building by building, and if necessary, annihilate its population. As the Spanish soldiers advanced into the city, they saw the evidence of disease and starvation. Mad with hunger, the Aztecs had gnawed the bark from trees. Bodies lay heaped in the streets. The once gleaming white city of the lakes had become a blackened ruin.

Cuauhtemoc is taken prisoner and brought before Cortes, who praised the Aztec leader for his bravery in battle.

Cortes, surrounded on all sides by Aztec warriors, narrowly escapes death. The Spaniards were caught off guard by the Aztecs' improved fighting techniques.

Seeing that the situation was hopeless, Cuauhtemoc fled Tenochtitlan in a canoe and was captured by a Spanish warship. Brought to Cortes as a prisoner, the last of the Aztec kings begged the captain-general to kill him with his dagger. Cortes refused, praised the young monarch's bravery, and issued orders to ensure that he and his people would be well treated. At Cuauhtemoc's command, the surviving Aztec warriors surrendered. Despite Cortes's orders, in parts of the city the Indian allies continued killing their traditional enemies, but by sundown a drizzling rain began and the city fell silent. It was August 13, 1521.

Chapter

9 "I Brought Your Majesty Kingdoms"

Incorporating Mexico into the Spanish empire would have been difficult enough if the Aztecs were Europeans, which they were not. Separated from Europe and Asia for thousands of years, the Indians were very different from their new overlords. To make matters worse, the wars between the Indians and the Spaniards had ravaged the countryside, destroying farms and towns. Now thousands starved. Tenochtitlan lay in ruins. Bodies littered the streets, threatening to add more disease to the plague that already stalked the city. Cortes immediately ordered his men to burn and bury the dead. Then in the chaos of his victory, the captain-general laid plans for governing his conquest—Mexico would become New Spain.

Cortes's men and their Indian allies cared less about Mexico's future than their own present. The Tlaxcalans sacked Tenochtitlan and took revenge on the

The battles between the Spaniards and Indians, depicted here, left the once beautiful city of Tenochtitlan in ruins. Cortes renamed Mexico New Spain, and made plans to rebuild the city.

An illustration portrays Indian slaves toiling in a Spanish mine. Many conquered Mexicans were forced into virtual slavery under the encomienda system implemented by Cortes.

hated Aztecs, killing as many as twelve thousand despite Cortes's orders to stop. Meanwhile, Spanish soldiers, tired of their captain-general's promises of future wealth, ransacked the city searching for Montezuma's treasure. Most of the gold and jewels captured in the conquest went to the king and to pay Cortes's expenses, however, leaving little booty for the common soldier—perhaps enough to buy a crossbow or a sword. At his men's insistence, Cortes had Cuauhtemoc tortured in an attempt to discover the location of the principal treasure but learned little. The soldiers knew their payment must come in a different form—land.

The Encomienda System

Without workers to cultivate the soil and develop the mines, the land would be useless. Spanish troops had captured thousands of Indians when Tenochtitlan fell, and Cortes ordered many of the prisoners branded and distributed as slaves among his men. The soldiers also expected to participate in the traditional Spanish encomienda system, under which the crown assigned to favored subjects parcels of land and the labor of Indians who lived on the grants but were not slaves, at least in theory. The people (*encomenderos*) holding the grants were supposed to allow "their" Indians to work for themselves most of the time, to protect them against abuse, and to instruct them in the Catholic faith. In practice, many encomenderos worked the Indians to death.

Seeing the Indian populations of Hispaniola and Cuba destroyed by the system, Cortes initially advised King Charles to abolish the encomienda system. As it happened, the king also thought the system might harm the Indians. When Cortes's men demanded payment for their service, however, the captain-general issued grants, and soon he began to fear that revoking the grants would cause the unruly soldiers to revolt, throwing New Spain into chaos. Determined to pacify his troops and to avoid Indian rebellion, the captain-general wrote to Charles again, explaining why New Spain in fact needed the encomienda system.

If the conquistadors were to obtain funds for their military service, he argued, they needed land and workers. Otherwise, the crown would have to pay the expenses. Under the soldiers' care, he added, the Indians would be protected and civilized. Charles eventually ordered Cortes to stop issuing grants under the encomienda system and to do away with those already in existence, but the captain-general, now the largest encomendero in the Americas, ignored the command.

King Charles (pictured) ordered Cortes to abolish the encomienda system in New Spain, but was defiantly ignored by the independent captain-general.

Cortes Seeks to Become Governor

The disagreement over the encomienda system was a sign of things to come. Charles admired Cortes but feared the conquistador was too independent. Velasquez and his allies constantly reinforced Charles's suspicions, reminding the king that Cortes had thrown off the governor's authority and might make New Spain a separate kingdom. In some ways, the captain-general already behaved like a king; he even built a magnificent residence for himself on the site of Montezuma's palace.

It was time to restrict this ambitious and dangerous man. Soon after the conquest, Spanish colonial authorities in Hispaniola sent Cristobal de Tapia to become New Spain's governor. Suspecting that Velasquez had arranged Tapia's appointment, Cortes welcomed this new competitor and treated him as a guest, but refused to accept his authority. Narvaez, who remained Cortes's prisoner, advised Tapia to take some gold from the captain-general and get out of New Spain while it was still possible. After a period of achieving nothing as governor, Tapia took Narvaez's advice, accepting a bribe from Cortes's representatives and abandoning his mission.

In an atmosphere of intrigue and uncertainty, Cortes continued to administer his conquest. He ordered the aqueducts to Mexico City rebuilt. He introduced European crops to New Spain. He brought in livestock and planned to improve the breeds. Expeditions searched the countryside for gold and silver mines. He sent Pedro de Alvarado and Cristobal de Olid to conquer Honduras and Guatemala and to search for a strait joining the Atlantic and Pacific Oceans, a task that had obsessed Spanish explorers and their Portuguese competitors for decades.

As always, Cortes strengthened his military forces. He bought weapons, munitions, and horses from Cuba and Spain. Anxious to make New Spain less dependent on imports, he produced his own gunpowder from native materials, on one occasion having his men lowered into a volcano's crater to get rocks containing sulfur. His men also located sources of tin, copper, and iron from which to cast their own cannon. If he had learned anything in the past four years, it was to prepare for all threats, Indian or Spanish.

A new threat soon appeared. The pesky governor of Jamaica, Francisco de Garay, returned to claim land as far north as the Rio Grande, a region Cortes had already settled. Driven out of Mexico once before by Cortes's men, the island governor now commanded 750 well-armed soldiers and a sixteen-ship fleet.

The captain-general soon learned of Garay's activities and led an army north to eliminate his competitor. Before the two armies met, a courier intercepted Cortes with a letter from Charles naming Cortes governor, captain-general, and chief justice of New Spain, which was defined to include land Garay had claimed. Faced with this document, Garay meekly surrendered his forces to Cortes and joined Narvaez as a prisoner in the new governor's residence. For the moment, the question of who ruled New Spain was settled.

Arguments in Favor of the Encomienda System

After initially arguing against establishing the encomienda system in New Spain, Cortes felt compelled by circumstances to reverse his opinion. In this extract from his third letter to Charles, Cortes explains why he has changed his mind.

"I informed Your Majesty how the natives of these parts are of much greater intelligence than those of . . . the islands; indeed, they appeared to us to possess . . . understanding . . . sufficient for an ordinary citizen to conduct himself in a civilized country. It seemed to me, therefore, a serious matter to compel them to serve the Spaniards . . . yet if this were not done, the conquerors and settlers of these parts would not be able to maintain themselves. . . . To avoid enslaving these Indians, and at the same time provide the Spaniards with their needs . . . I have been almost forced to deliver the chieftains and other natives . . . to the Spaniards in recognition of the services they have rendered to Your Majesty . . . because . . . we have been at war a long time and have all contracted debts."

With his political authority established by royal decree, Cortes turned his attention to the Indians' spiritual needs. Soon after the conquest, he had requested that the crown send friars to convert the Indians to Catholicism. In May 1524, twelve Franciscan friars arrived in Mexico. The Indians, accustomed to armor-clad Spanish conquistadors lusting after gold, were amazed to see the friars, dressed in the rough dark robes of their order, trudging barefoot from the coast to the rebuilt capital, now called Mexico City. The Indians were equally astonished to see Cortes, whom many Indians considered a god, meet the friars with gifts, remove his cap before them, and kneel to kiss the hems of their robes. The act was deliberate. The conqueror of Mexico, Malinche, wanted the Indians to copy his reverence toward the servants of God. Impressed by their new ruler's example, the Indians showed remarkable willingness to become Catholics.

Cortes in Honduras

The challenges of ruling both Indians and Spaniards distracted Cortes from spiritual matters. In the summer of 1524, he learned that Olid, having abandoned his search for a strait to the Pacific, had appointed officials for Honduras, imprisoned some of Cortes's friends, and killed some Spaniards. In short, Olid had committed serious crimes and now acted as governor of a new colony, much as Cortes had ignored Velasquez.

Cortes reacted much as Velasquez had. He hastily dispatched an expedition to bring Olid to justice, but then decided to

A Spanish priest performs a baptism in New Spain. Many of the Indians displayed a surprising willingness to convert to Catholicism.

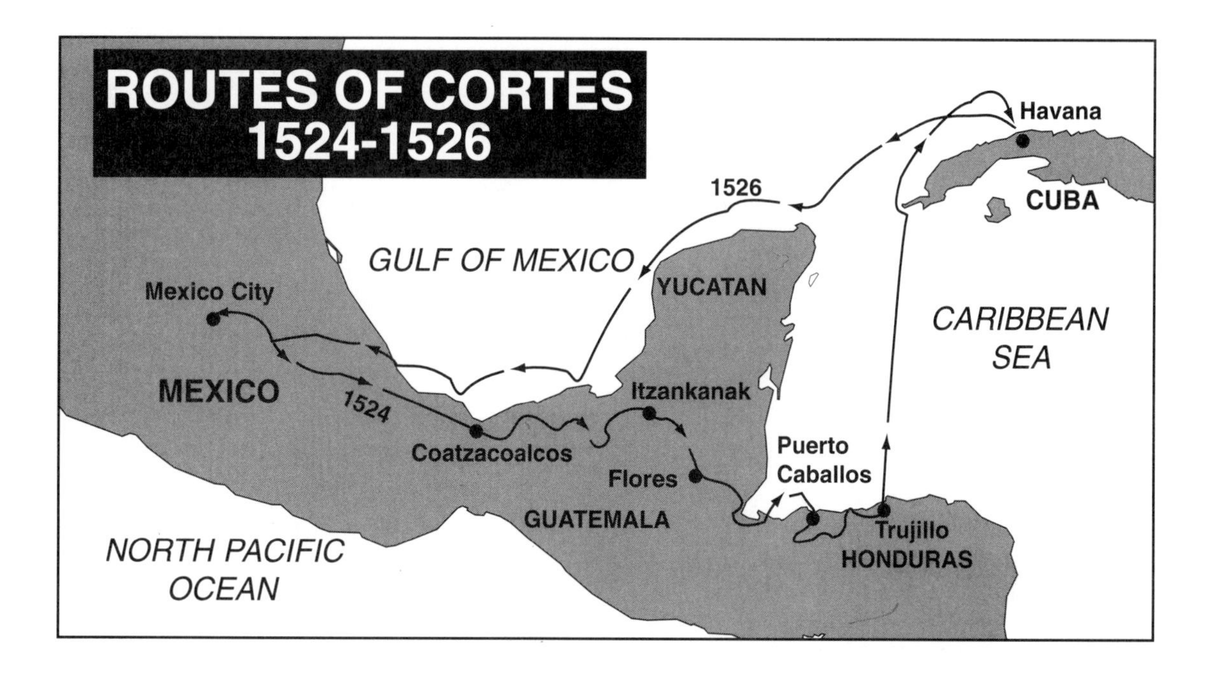

deal with the problem personally. Besides, he hoped to discover and conquer cities with even greater wealth than those in Mexico. Fearing that his absence would invite rebellion in Mexico, Cortes's lieutenants begged him not to go, but the captain-general ignored them. Olid had to be punished as an example to others who might challenge his authority. Cortes should have listened to his officers.

In some ways the achievements of Hernando Cortes in the Central American jungles surpassed the conquest of Mexico, but the expedition that began in 1524 brought him little glory or gold. Although he conquered some towns, none were as large or as rich as those in Mexico. In Honduras, Cortes conquered the jungle. For months, the Spaniards hovered on the edge of starvation, eating little more than roots and herbs. The conquistadors used their swords more often against jungle undergrowth than against hostile Indians. Often rivers blocked their way, and Cortes had to build fifty wooden bridges, some as long as three hundred meters. One soldier, driven mad by fever and hunger, fled screaming into the forest and disappeared forever.

His strength sapped by near-starvation and overexertion, Cortes again faced the threat of rebellion. To ensure that the Mexican Indians would remain peaceful in his absence, he had taken Cuauhtemoc and his nobles on the journey as hostages. An Indian told Cortes that the Aztec king intended to kill the weakened Spaniards and call on his people to rebel. Cortes interrogated the Aztecs separately, and each, believing the Spaniard could magically read their minds, confessed to involvement in the plot. The captain-general had Cuauhtemoc and two of his nobles hanged. Little did he know that as he crushed one rebellion in the jungle, another had broken out in Mexico.

Having reached the Honduran coast at Trujillo, Cortes and the other survivors

Cortes's Decision to Execute Cuauhtemoc

While Gomara rarely criticizes the conqueror of Mexico (who was also his employer), in Cortes *he does condemn the execution of Cuauhtemoc.*

"Cuauhtemoc was . . . a valiant man, and in every adversity proved his royal heart and courage, in favor of peace at the beginning of the war, and in perseverance during the siege. . . . Cortes should have preserved his life as a precious jewel, for Cuauhtemoc was the triumph and glory of his victories; but Cortes did not wish to keep him alive in such a troubled land and time. It is true that he thought highly of him and that the Indians held him in the same honor and reverence in which they held Moctezuma; and I believe it was for this reason that Cortes always had Cuauhtemoc in his company when he rode through the city, or went on foot."

of the expedition to the east of the Yucatan Peninsula learned that Olid had already been arrested and executed. The mission that had cost so many lives had been pointless. Worse, the officials Cortes had entrusted with Mexico's government had declared him dead, confiscated his property, ransacked his home, tortured one of his kinsmen in an attempt to locate Montezuma's treasure, and abused the Indians.

Despite his weakened condition, Cortes intended to march to Mexico City and punish the rebels. Before his departure, however, he received word that his allies had already imprisoned the remaining members. With New Spain now at peace, Cortes started for the capital at a more leisurely pace, arriving in May 1526. Thin and sick, he made his way to the town of Medellin (modern-day Veracruz), sent messengers informing the neighboring towns of his arrival, and entered a church to offer prayers of thanks for his safety.

The news of Cortes's return created a holiday atmosphere. When Cortes approached the capital, Gomara wrote, the city's population gave him a thunderous welcome:

> His entrance into Mexico [City] was the occasion for the greatest . . . jubilation. . . . All the Spaniards . . . sallied forth in military array, while Indians flocked to see him as if he had been Moctezuma himself. They filled the streets to overflowing; they showed their joy by dancing, by the beating of drums and the blowing of conches . . . and many fifes; and all that day and night they surged through the streets making bonfires. . . . At that time Cortes was the most famous man of our nation.[29]

Jealous of Cortes's wealth and fame, Velasquez tried to convince the king that the conqueror of New Spain had hidden Montezuma's treasure for himself and was rebellious. Cortes did his best to gain Charles's favor. Before leaving for Honduras, Cortes had sent the king a treasure shipment including a magnificent cannon cast entirely from Mexican silver. The gifts arrived just as Charles considered removing Cortes from all his offices because of the serious accusations against him. Impressed by the shipment, Charles decided merely to send an official, Luis Ponce de Leon, to investigate Cortes's activities during his years in Mexico.

Ponce de Leon arrived in 1526, just as Cortes returned from Honduras, and in the king's name replaced the captain-general as chief justice of New Spain and stripped him of his offices. Although Cortes considered the investigation insulting, he welcomed the new chief justice as a guest in his own home. Soon afterward, Ponce de Leon died, apparently of yellow fever or another tropical illness. Before Ponce de Leon died, he named a successor as chief justice; but within two months, the successor also died. To make matters worse, Garay, still in Cortes's custody, and Cortes's wife, Catalina, who had joined her husband in Mexico, died as well. Although all four probably died of fever, the deaths of four people in Cortes's home during a relatively short time looked suspicious. Velasquez and his allies eagerly spread the rumor that all had been poisoned by the captain-general.

Cortes Appeals to the King

Cortes found himself in a confusing situation. Temporarily appointed captain-general by the last chief justice, he now

Returning from a two-year expedition to Honduras, Cortes receives a joyous welcome from the residents of Mexico City.

faced yet another chief justice, Alonso de Estrada. Estrada promptly exiled the conqueror of New Spain from Mexico City. Smarting at this latest insult, Cortes withdrew to his summer palace at Coyoacan on the southern shore of the lake. Although he lived in grand style, the captain-general grew weary of his forced retirement. Cortes decided to take his grievances directly to the king and sailed for Spain on March 17, 1528.

By now the most talked-about man in the nation, Cortes dazzled Spain with the wonders of the New World. Aztec nobles in their brilliant feather robes humbly attended him as they had Montezuma. Indian acrobats performed feats of agility so amazing that they later were invited to travel to Italy to perform for the pope. Cortes displayed for the amusement of the court exotic American animals including an opossum and an armadillo. Of course, he brought the usual gifts of gold and jewels for his king.

Although New Spain had become the center of Cortes's life, it was merely a profitable sideshow to Charles, who was looking forward to his coronation as emperor of the Holy Roman Empire, a vast domain stretching from the Baltic to the Mediterranean Sea. (Although Charles had been elected to head the Holy Roman Empire in 1519, he was not crowned by the pope until 1530.) In addition, events in South America distracted the European ruler, and Francisco Pizarro had arrived at court, asking permission to conquer Peru, a land many believed would prove even richer than New Spain.

When Cortes finally met Charles in autumn, the king received him graciously. The son of a poor Estremaduran noble,

Cortes sailed for Spain in 1528 laden with gifts of gold and jewels for the king and accompanied by Aztec nobles, Indian acrobats, and exotic American animals. Among the most interesting creatures he brought for exhibit were an opossum (left) and an armadillo (right).

Cortes Sends for Missionaries

Cortes admired much in the Indians' moral code. In this portion of his fourth letter to Charles, he urges the king to send as missionaries low-ranking churchmen who were morally and spiritually upright to serve as good examples to Spain's newest subjects.

"If we have bishops and other dignitaries, they will only follow the customs of squandering the goods of the Church on pomp and ceremony, and other vices. . . . And the evil here would be still greater, for the natives . . . had in their time religious persons . . . who were so severe in the observance both of chastity and honesty that if any one of them was held by anyone to have transgressed he was put to death. If these people were now to see . . . [church] dignitaries . . . indulge in the vices and profanities now common in Spain . . . it would bring our faith into much contempt. . . . This would cause such harm that I believe any further preaching would be of no avail."

Cortes now sat next to the king at mass. When he fell ill and lay near death, Charles visited his bedside, an act unheard of for the Spanish ruler. Once he had recovered, Cortes traveled with Charles, explaining his complaints and recommending policies for the administration of New Spain. In July 1529, the king declared Cortes captain-general of New Spain and marquess of the Valley of Oaxaca. As marquess, Cortes became a great lord with the power to rule twenty-three thousand Indians and dozens of towns. Covering twenty-five thousand square miles, his Mexican realm was larger than some European kingdoms and made him one of the richest men on earth.

It was not enough. Against all odds, Cortes had conquered New Spain. Now he felt entitled to govern the empire he had given his king; but Charles intended to increase his own power, not give it away to an independent-minded warrior. In fact, Spanish colonial authorities had already sent a new commission to take over government of New Spain. Its officers not only had not fought alongside Cortes in the conquest, they were supporters of Velasquez. Worse, these men would continue the investigation into the captain-general's dealings.

Charles urged Cortes to accept his changed circumstances and soothed the conquistador's bruised ego with a charter to conquer any lands that touched the Pacific Ocean. After all, were not there rumors of lands richer than Mexico to the west? Unable to settle political matters satisfactorily, Cortes turned his attention to affairs of the heart. Some of Cortes's friends arranged a marriage between the widowed conquistador and Doña Juana de Zuñiga, the beautiful young daughter of a Spanish count. Hopelessly in love, the new marquess gave his lady five priceless emeralds, delicately carved by Indian craftsmen.

In the spring of 1530, Cortes sailed for Mexico with his bride, his titles and honors, and no real power to rule anything beyond his estate. When he arrived in Mexico in July, the population gave him a triumphal welcome. The Indians complained that the new governor, Nuño de Guzman, had taken their food and sold thousands of people into slavery in the Caribbean islands. Many begged Cortes to join revolts against the new government, but he refused and settled in the city of Texcoco, still exiled from the capital. Unable to suppress the rebellions triggered by Guzman's abusive policies, the commission persuaded the captain-general to lead an expedition to restore peace. In the minds of the Indians, Malinche was the only real ruler of New Spain. It was an opinion the crown did not share.

In response to intense dissatisfaction among the people, Spanish colonial authorities replaced Guzman's oppressive government with a new commission, which still did not include Cortes. Snubbed again, the captain-general turned to what he knew best—exploration. Inspired in part by legends of islands inhabited by women warrior Amazons rich with gold, Cortes had ships built on Mexico's west coast. From 1532 to 1539 his vessels explored the west coast of Mexico and also discovered California's southern peninsula. Plagued by storms, mutiny, hostile Indians, and shipwreck, the expeditions found no rich new lands, no great cities, and no Amazons.

In 1535 Cortes sailed with a fleet to the Gulf of California (for a time called the Sea of Cortes). Although he fared no better than had his lieutenants, the old conquistador once again proved himself to be a master of resourcefulness. On one occasion he and his men rebuilt a ship

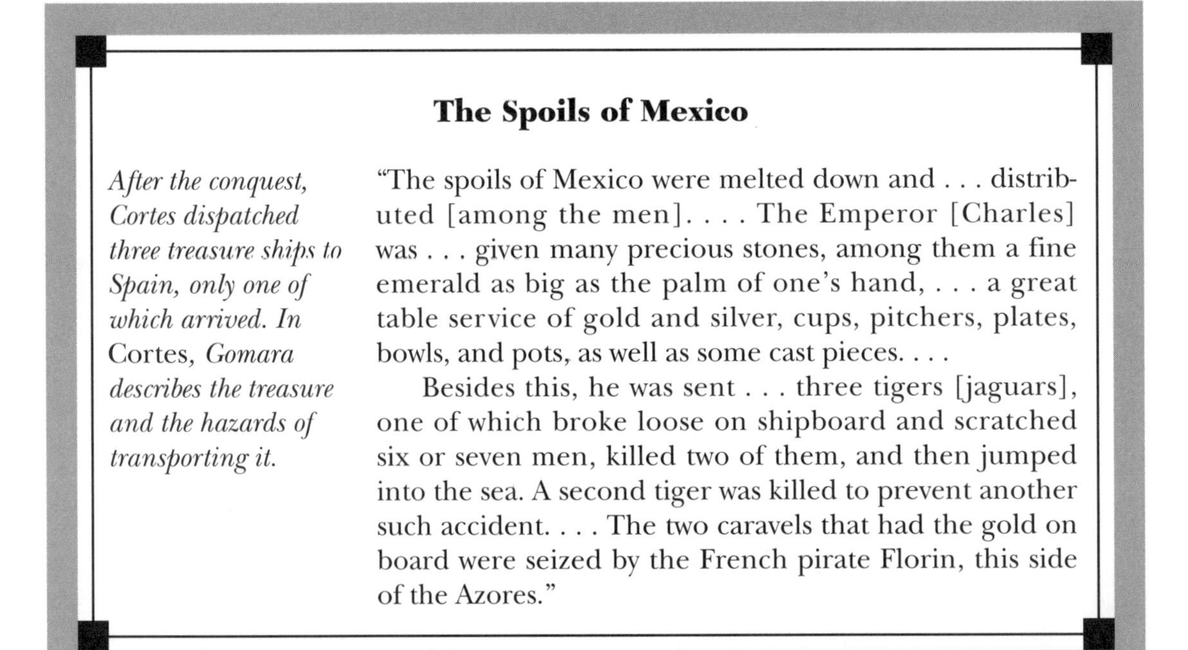

The Spoils of Mexico

After the conquest, Cortes dispatched three treasure ships to Spain, only one of which arrived. In Cortes, *Gomara describes the treasure and the hazards of transporting it.*

"The spoils of Mexico were melted down and . . . distributed [among the men]. . . . The Emperor [Charles] was . . . given many precious stones, among them a fine emerald as big as the palm of one's hand, . . . a great table service of gold and silver, cups, pitchers, plates, bowls, and pots, as well as some cast pieces. . . .

Besides this, he was sent . . . three tigers [jaguars], one of which broke loose on shipboard and scratched six or seven men, killed two of them, and then jumped into the sea. A second tiger was killed to prevent another such accident. . . . The two caravels that had the gold on board were seized by the French pirate Florin, this side of the Azores."

from wreckage so they could return to New Spain; but a conquistador gained no glory from mere survival. Cortes had spent a fortune on the quest and had found nothing. In frustration, one of his captains named a point on the California peninsula "Cape Disappointment." For Cortes there would be no more Mexicos.

More Disappointments

One last hope remained. In July 1536, Alvar Nuñez Cabeza de Vaca and three starving companions stumbled into Mexico City, the only survivors of the exploration of the unknown regions north of Mexico led by the bumbling Panfilo de Narvaez. Crossing what is now the southwestern United States, the explorers reported native stories of cities and kingdoms in the lands above Mexico. These lands, thought Cortes, should be his to explore and claim.

Stripped of his title as governor of New Spain, Cortes set out in search of rich new lands to explore. To his dismay, the expeditions resulted in little more than disappointment.

Cortes pressed Antonio de Mendoza, the recently appointed viceroy (an official second only to the king) of New Spain, to send him on an expedition to the north. Knowing Cortes's talents and temperament all too well, Mendoza sent a Franciscan friar, Marcus of Nice, to explore the unknown lands. When Marcus returned from his expedition telling tales of the Seven Cities of Cibola, where Indians used gold for common utensils, Cortes hounded Mendoza again for authorization to conquer the land. The viceroy still refused and instead appointed twenty-nine-year-old Vasquez de Coronado, the governor of the Mexican province of New Galicia, to undertake the mission. Mendoza had already angered Cortes by ruling that his estate was smaller than the marquess claimed. Now furious that the viceroy had denied him command again, Cortes and two of his sons sailed for Spain in January 1540. Once more, he would take his complaints to the king.

When Cortes reached Spain, Charles was preparing an attack on Algiers and had no interest in settling quarrels among his nobles. Cortes organized a unit of cavalry at his own expense and joined the African expedition, but nearly drowned when a storm in the Mediterranean wrecked the entire fleet. As the old warrior stumbled onto the beach, he realized that his wife's five great emeralds, which he had carried for safekeeping in a bag around his neck, were now at the bottom of the sea with Charles's fleet.

The Conqueror's Death

Early in this century, American and western European historians often admired Cortes. Henry Morton Robinson's description of the conqueror's death in Stout Cortez: A Biography of the Spanish Conquest, *serves as an example.*

"Cortez was not unwilling to die. He was sixty-two years old, a ripe age indeed for a sixteenth century conquistador. He had outlived the chief companions of his great period, and had seen his principal enemies . . . die long before him. A new generation of conquerors had sprung up to eclipse his fame; his early triumphs were fading from the memories of living men. There was nothing left to struggle or hope for. . . . And so at length, after a futile rally, the hero of a thousand armed attacks, the survivor of a score of shipwrecks, and the lifelong challenger of violence, died peacefully in his bed . . . after receiving the last rites of the religion he had so ardently served."

The Spanish commanders, without consulting Cortes, decided to give up the attack because the storm had reduced their numbers and left them short of supplies. Amazed at their timidity, the marquess boldly promised that he would take the city if they would give him a small force. After all, he had taken Tenochtitlan against much greater odds. He was ignored. The army returned to Spain, beaten by a storm.

Cortes clung to the hope that Charles would give him Mexico to rule again, but in six years, he saw the king only briefly. Mexico and its conqueror were old news. For the hero of Spain, the god of Mexico, no punishment surpassed being forgotten. In *Conquistadors in North American History*, historian Paul Horgan relates a legend that illustrates the conqueror's fate.

> One day in the street . . . [Cortes] saw the royal carriage approaching, and in desperation he threw himself upon it, clinging to its straps and calling to its occupant.
>
> "Who is this man?" asked Charles. . . .
>
> "I am the man," cried Hernando Cortes, "who brought to Your Majesty more kingdoms than your father left you towns!"
>
> The coach swept on. Cortes was swallowed up by the street crowds.[30]

Old and sick, Cortes prepared to sail for New Spain to spend his last days. There, at least, he might enjoy one last triumphal return. But before the former captain-general could board his ship, he became too ill to continue the journey. Having cheated death so often, the old warrior knew his time had come. On December 2, 1547, Malinche died in the land where the sun rises.

Cortes's Legacy

For nearly five centuries, Cortes's reputation has swung between extremes. In his lifetime, he was seen as an irresponsible romantic, a wealthy colonial landlord, and the most heroic figure of his generation; he died a forgotten old man. Cortes saw himself as the man who had conquered kingdoms in a righteous cause, enriched his king (and himself), and saved the souls of millions. Now he is regarded as the destroyer of cultures.

Cortes's conquests had a lasting, but largely negative, impact on Spain and Mexico.

Cortes's Impact on Spain

It is true that Cortes gave Spain her first great fortune, but that fortune bankrupted her. Silver and gold from the mines of Mexico (and then Peru) flooded the world market, causing inflation (rising prices) across Europe. By 1598, despite the bounty of her American mines and plantations, Spain's massive military spending had put the country deeply in debt. By 1700 her industries lagged behind her English and Dutch competitors, her neglected farms produced less than they had in 1500, and her military establishment had slipped into second-rate status. Cortes never dreamed that the spoils he sent his king would be so uselessly squandered.

Cortes's Impact on Mexico

If Mexican treasure proved a mixed blessing for Spain, it created a romantic vision of the New World that endures to this day. For decades after Cortes's conquests, Spanish adventurers searched for another Mexico. Aside from Pizarro in Peru, none found one. Nevertheless, America became

Young children play around a filthy, stagnant pool in a Mexico City slum. Ironically, the "golden land" that once beckoned countless explorers to its coasts now suffers high unemployment and chronic poverty.

known as a golden land. Ironically, the country in which the myth of golden America was born today suffers chronic poverty. Mexico constantly has high unemployment and low per capita income and still endures the sort of inflation Aztec gold unleashed on the world centuries ago.

The encomienda Cortes granted in Mexico set the pattern for conflicts over landownership that still plague the country. Throughout Mexican history, a few men have owned huge estates, leaving little land for the rest of the population—a situation that has helped cause revolutions and economic hardship in the country. The conquerors described Mexico as a land of productive, well-ordered fields and beautiful cities. Undoubtedly the Spaniards failed to report much existing poverty and suffering, but even so, one cannot help won-

Cortes the Deliverer

In the early twentieth century, writers were often less concerned with preserving cultures than civilizing them according to the Western, Christian standards. Accordingly, in Blood Drenched Altars, *published in 1935, Francis Clement Kelly portrays Cortes positively.*

"Cortes has been . . . vigorously condemned for his methods of conquest. Little, however, is said of his . . . genuine statesmanship and his determination . . . to Christianize the New World. . . . His Indian policy put him centuries ahead of his time, and the policy worked, unlike the many adopted by the colonizers of the north.

This 'oppressor of the Indians' seemed oftenest to be considered by them as a friend. . . . The truth is that Cortes was looked upon by the tribes opposed to the Aztecs as their deliverer from a bloody tyranny. . . .

Had there been no invasion of European civilization into America . . . the whole continent would have become the home of primitive . . . tribes practicing gross idolatry and cannibalism."

dering whether Cortes brought economic ruin to a rich country or merely hastened the destruction of a system that would have collapsed anyway.

The Spanish Legacy in Mexico

As for the Mexicans, Cortes helped to create a new people. From the beginning, the conquistadors married native women. Marina bore Cortes's favorite son, and for generations after the conquest, the nobles of Mexico included descendants of Aztec chieftains. Today, over 60 percent of the Mexican population is considered mestizo (mixed Spanish and Indian heritage). Roughly one-tenth are considered Caucasian (white). Spanish America became a much more racially blended society than English or French America ever did, and this homogenization began with Cortes and the chieftains who chose to become his allies.

Many of the Central American chieftains and their people became Christians because of Cortes's insistence. Although he often used heavy-handed means to persuade the Indians to convert, today 97 percent of all Mexicans are considered Catholics. Nevertheless, one legacy of forced conversion centuries ago is a tradition of deep hostility in some parts of the population, including especially the leaders of Mexico's many revolutions, to whom the church represents European domination of Native Americans. But the Catholic Church in Mexico is not entirely European. In rural areas, peasants still burn incense before stone idols, who now bear the names of saints instead of Indian deities.

Clearly, native culture survived attempts by Cortes and other Spaniards to erase it. Tourists to Cozumel can see Mayan dances before the bullfights begin. The rural poor still live in many ways much as their Mayan and Aztec ancestors did. The native people of Mexico, however, lost much of their heritage. While some priests and friars such as Sahagun preserved Indian manuscripts, far more of these valuable documents were burned. Indian artwork was destroyed, and temples flattened. Cortes and those who followed came to reshape Mexico and its people,

Although often accomplished by force, the conversion of the Indians to Christianity was hugely successful. Today Catholicism is practiced by 97 percent of all Mexicans.

not to adapt to them. The process was well advanced by the end of the sixteenth century, according to C. W. Ceram: "Aztec culture was already dead and all but forgotten some eighty years after Cortes had struck into its vitals. The . . . Aztecs . . . still living in Mexico today exist . . . in a historical vacuum."[31]

Because of Cortes's conquest of Mexico, the Indians lost not only knowledge of their past; many lost their lives, as well. Las Casas claimed that millions died through warfare and disease. Although the Spanish missionary was known to exaggerate, especially in accounts concerning Cortes's exploits, modern scholars say that in the sixteenth century, as much as 70 percent of the population died as a result of disease. Thousands died from the years of war that followed Cortes's arrival, and many from overwork in slavery, but actual numbers are difficult to determine.

Certainly, Cortes saw hundreds die daily during the construction of Mexico City. In his biography of the conqueror, Gomara described Cortes's determination to rebuild the capital despite the costs in human lives:

> [Cortes] strove to make [Tenochtitlan/Mexico City] greater and more populous than it had been. . . . To reduce the expense of building, he brought in a number of Indians. . . . He distributed and promised homesites . . . and other privileges to the natives of Mexico and to all who would come and settle there. . . . Upon hearing that Mexico-Tenochtitlan was being rebuilt, and that the citizens were to be free . . . many people came. . . . They worked so hard and ate so little that they sickened, the pestilence [plague] attacked them, and an infinite number died. The work was heavy, because they had to carry in on their backs, or drag, the stone, earth, lumber, lime, bricks, and all other materials. Nevertheless, their songs and music, their invocations of their city and lord . . . were something to hear. The shortage of food was caused by

An illustration of seventeenth-century Mexico City while under Spanish rule. Tragically, thousands of Indian slaves were worked to death while rebuilding the city.

Cortes put an end to the abhorred Aztec practice of human sacrifice, depicted here. He claimed that the lives he spared by ending this practice justified the lives lost during the construction of Mexico City.

> the [recent] siege and war, during which they could not plant as they customarily did.[32]

The captain-general felt that the deaths of the Indian workers were more than offset by his well-enforced decree ending human sacrifice. In the first two decades of the sixteenth century, the Aztecs sometimes sacrificed thousands of victims in a single day. If anything, human sacrifice was becoming more common in the region, not less. Had the practice continued across all of Mexico for generations, the slaughter would have been incredible.

Cortes anticipated the deaths that might result from Spanish contact with the Indians and attempted to protect the native people from the worst effects of such intermingling. It is interesting that the Indians who knew Cortes saw him as a savior and source of justice. It was the generations that followed that regarded him as the slaughterer of Aztec hordes, the first of the European oppressors in Mexico.

Certainly Cortes saw himself as a liberator of the Indians, and without abandoning his personal greed and ambition, he attempted to make Mexico prosperous for Spaniard and Indian alike. Above all, he intended to avoid the waste and destruction that Spanish colonization had brought to Hispaniola and Cuba. His fifth letter to Charles describes his concerns for the people he governed:

> As it is my duty to make the best arrangements I am able for the colonization of this land, and so that the natives and the Spanish settlers may maintain themselves and prosper, and Our Holy Catholic Faith take root, . . . I issued certain ordinances [rules]. Some of the Spaniards who reside in these parts are not entirely satisfied with some of them . . . for most of them expect to do with these lands as was done in the [Caribbean] Islands when they were colonized, that is, to harvest, destroy and then abandon them. And . . . it seems to me that it would be unpardonable for those of us who have had experience in the past not to do better.[33]

While the Indians of Mexico avoided the wholesale annihilation suffered by the natives of Hispaniola and Cuba, they were not spared the hardships of colonization.

Even at the end of his life, Cortes found himself preoccupied with the Indians' welfare. On his deathbed Cortes the slave-owner asked one of his sons to consider freeing Mexico's Indian slaves. The natives' plight cannot be wholly laid at Cortes's feet, since he never had a free hand to develop Mexico as he saw fit.

Cortes the Conqueror

If the Spaniards had not arrived first, it is probable that other Europeans would have conquered Mexico eventually. The people of Mexico had captured or driven away three Spanish expeditions before 1519, but Cortes conquered Mexico by a combination of cunning and sheer force of will. The details of the conquistador's early life, though sketchy, still tell us something about why he succeeded where others failed. Born physically weak, he challenged his body until it became powerful. The child of a family whose poverty mocked their noble ancestry, he struggled to make himself wealthy. Born to a hard, barren, unyielding region, he made himself master of a land that was as visually stunning as it was rich. Reared in obscurity, he made himself the most famous man of his generation. In Cortes, adversity bred ambition, and obstacles became opportunities.

Underlying all was his abiding confidence in God and in his patron, Saint Peter, whom he believed had saved him from death in childhood. Thus Cortes remained a risk taker his entire life. To him death by mishap and defeat were unthinkable, and at every turn he willingly gambled everything in the hope of gaining power, fame, and glory. Surely, every narrow escape

Indians resist a Spanish expedition. Cortes's strong will and craftiness enabled him to succeed at conquering Mexico where others had failed.

Cortes the Destroyer

Writing in the 1970s, J. H. Plumb, in his introduction to William Weber Johnson's Cortes, *emphasizes the conquistador's destructive effect on Mexico.*

"Diseases—particularly smallpox—brought in by the Spaniards decimated [greatly reduced] the population. The ruthless savagery of their new conquerors killed far more than the sacrifices demanded by the Aztecs, and one of the most populous and fertile valleys of the world lost both its people and its vitality. . . . Mercilessly exploited, totally subjected, Mexico became Spanish and Christian; irradicably [unalterably] so, no matter how blended with cultural strains from the Aztec past.

Cortes, of course, is no longer a Mexican hero. . . . Yet the result of [the] conquest still reverberates—Spanish is the language, and at the great shrine of Guadalupe one may see . . . the rapt Indian faces, lost in prayer to the Madonna."

from death, and every triumph, only convinced him of the rightness of his course.

A Symbol of European Domination

In 1823, when Mexico broke away from Spanish rule, some of the anti-European revolutionary leaders planned to celebrate by destroying Cortes's remains, which had been moved to Mexico. Cortes's descendants learned of these plans and moved the coffin before the revolutionaries arrived. The body remained hidden for over a century, being rediscovered in 1946 in an abandoned church. The Mexican government ordered Cortes's remains reburied in the same place and declared the building a national monument. Malinche sleeps in the land he created.

ALAMEDA FREE LIBRARY

Notes

Introduction: A Sixteenth-Century Hero

1. Francisco Lopez de Gomara, *Cortes: The Life of the Conqueror.* Translated and edited by Lesley Byrd Simpson. Los Angeles: University of California Press, 1964.
2. Bartolomé de Las Casas, *Tears of the Indians.* Translated by Sir Arthur Helps. Williamstown, MA: John Lilburne Company, 1970.

Chapter 1: The Call of Adventure

3. Hammond Innes, *The Conquistadors.* New York: Knopf, 1969.
4. Gomara, *Cortes.*
5. Las Casas, *Tears of the Indians.*

Chapter 2: The Captain-General

6. Quoted in Bernal Diaz [del Castillo], *The Conquest of New Spain.* Translated by J. M. Cohen. New York: Penguin Classics, 1976.
7. Diaz, *The Conquest of New Spain.*
8. William H. Prescott, *Conquest of Mexico.* New York: Book League of America, 1843, 1934.
9. Quoted in Gomara, *Cortes.*
10. Diaz, *The Conquest of New Spain.*
11. Quoted in Diaz, *The Conquest of New Spain.*

Chapter 3: Into Battle

12. Diaz, *The Conquest of New Spain.*
13. Gomara, *Cortes.*

Chapter 4: The Return of the Gods

14. Bernal Diaz del Castillo, *The Discovery and Conquest of Mexico: 1517–1521.* Translated by A. P. Maudslay. New York: Farrar, Straus, and Cudahy, 1956.
15. Gomara, *Cortes.*
16. Diaz, *The Discovery and Conquest of Mexico.*

Chapter 5: Tlaxcala

17. Gomara, *Cortes.*
18. Diaz, *The Discovery and Conquest of Mexico.*

Chapter 6: The Land of Enchantment

19. Quoted in Gomara, *Cortes.*
20. Diaz, *The Discovery and Conquest of Mexico.*
21. Diaz, *The Discovery and Conquest of Mexico.*
22. Quoted in Gomara, *Cortes.*
23. Diaz, *The Discovery and Conquest of Mexico.*

Chapter 7: The Sorrowful Night

24. Quoted in Diaz, *The Discovery and Conquest of Mexico.*
25. Hernando Cortes, *Hernan Cortes: Letters from Mexico.* Translated by A. R. Pagden. New York: Grossman Publishers, 1971.
26. Gomara, *Cortes.*

Chapter 8: The Return to Tenochtitlan

27. Prescott, *Conquest of Mexico.*
28. Cortes, *Letters.*

Chapter 9: "I Brought Your Majesty Kingdoms"

29. Gomara, *Cortes.*
30. Paul Horgan, *Conquistadors in North American History.* Greenwich, CT: Fawcett Publications, 1965.

Epilogue: Cortes's Legacy

31. C. W. Ceram, *Gods, Graves, and Scholars: The Story of Archaeology.* New York: Bantam Books, 1972.
32. Gomara, *Cortes.*
33. Cortes, *Letters.*

For Further Reading

Mortimer Adler, ed., *The Annals of America, 1493–1754*, vol. 1. Chicago: William Benton, Publisher, Encyclopaedia Britannica, 1968. This multivolume set provides a sampling of documents important to American history from the colonial era to the 1960s.

Maurice Boyd, *Tabascan Myths & Legends*. Fort Worth: Texas Christian University Press, 1969. This relatively unknown book offers insights into the beliefs of the first mainland Indians Cortes encountered.

Caesar C. Cantu, *Cortes and the Fall of the Aztec Empire*. Los Angeles: Modern World Publishing Company, 1966. Emphasizes the importance of the Indians in making Cortes's conquest of Mexico possible.

Frederick F. Cartwright, *Disease and History*. New York: New American Library, 1972. A remarkable little book detailing instances in which disease has influenced the course of world events. Provides staggering figures of Indian depopulation due to European diseases.

Maurice Collis, *Cortes and Montezuma*. New York: Harcourt, Brace, and Company, 1954. A scholarly account of attempts by conqueror and king to manipulate each other. Thoroughly researched; one of the standard biographies.

William Weber Johnson, *Mexico*. New York: Time Incorporated, 1961. Only partly devoted to Cortes and the conquest, but incorporates excellent anecdotal information on Cortes and the way Mexicans view him today.

F. A. Kirkpatrick, *The Spanish Conquistadors*. New York: World Publishing Company, 1962. A balanced account of Cortes, his accomplishments, his strengths, and his weaknesses.

Hilde Krueger, *Malinche, or Farewell to Myths*. New York: Arrowhead Press Book for Storm Publishers, 1948. This little book focuses mainly on Marina but reaches the intriguing conclusion that the Indians considered Cortes and his interpreter a god comprised of two beings.

Bartolomé de las Casas, *The Devastation of the Indies: A Brief Account*. Translated by Hermé Briffault. Baltimore: Johns Hopkins University Press, 1992. *History of the Indies*. Translated by Andrée Collard. New York: Harper & Row, 1971. Las Casas wrote vivid, and sometimes imaginative, descriptions of Spanish abuse of the Indians throughout the Caribbean. Once Cortes's friend, he became one of the conqueror's most outspoken critics.

———, *The Life of Las Casas*. Translated by Sir Arthur Helps. Williamstown, MA: John Lilburne Company, 1970. With some variations, Las Casas's account is hostile to the conquistadors in general and to Cortes in particular. While valuable for its description of atrocities against the Indians, the work is flawed because it is often based on hearsay.

Bart MacDowell, "The Aztecs," *National Geographic*, December 1980. This account of Aztec culture and history is enhanced by stunning artists' conceptions of the Aztec people and their capital.

Richard Lee Marks, *Cortes: The Great Adventurer and the Fate of Aztec Mexico*. New York: Knopf, 1993. Bluntly describes Cortes's moral shortcomings, but surprising sympathy is shown for the great conquistador.

Michael C. Meyer and William L. Sherman, *The Course of Mexican History*. New York: Oxford University Press, 1979. General background information on Mexico during and after the conquest.

Eduardo Matos Moctezuma, "The Great Temple," *National Geographic*, December 1980. This article by a writer who shares the Aztec king's name examines the structure that dominated Tenochtitlan and served as a battleground for the Spaniards and the Aztec people.

August F. Molina Montes, "Tenochtitlan's Glory," *National Geographic*, December 1980. Helps the reader understand the awe the Aztec capital inspired in the conquistadors.

Henry Bamford Parkes, *A History of Mexico*. Boston: Houghton Mifflin, 1960. Includes a good account of Cortes's conflicts with the other conquistadors and Spanish bureaucrats who came to Mexico.

Lesley Byrd Simpson, *The Encomienda in New Spain: The Beginning of Spanish Mexico*. Los Angeles: University of California Press, 1966. Describes Cortes's legal problems after the conquest, events often neglected or glossed over in Cortes biographies.

Hudson Strode, *Timeless Mexico*. New York: Harcourt, Brace, and Company, 1944. Includes a segment on the Quetzalcoatl myth that helps the reader understand Montezuma's confusion in dealing with Cortes.

Gene S. Stuart, *The Mighty Aztecs*. Washington, DC: Special Publications Division, National Geographic Society, 1981. Well illustrated and highly readable; provides a colorful look at the great military and political power of Cortes's adversaries.

Alpheus Hyatt Verrill, *Great Conquerors of South and Central America*. New York: New Home Library, 1929. Writing at a time when some of the great European empires still existed and were considered a civilizing influence in the world, Verrill concluded that Cortes was remarkably humane in his conduct toward conquered people.

Victor Wolfgang von Hagen, *The Aztec: Man and Tribe*. New York: New American Library, 1962. A compact but thorough description of the culture Cortes destroyed.

S. Jeffrey K. Wilkerson, "Following Cortes: Path to Conquest," *National Geographic*, October 1984. Thanks to colorful illustrations, this article gives the reader a chance to visualize events much as Cortes saw them.

Works Consulted

C. W. Ceram, *Gods, Graves, and Scholars: The Story of Archaeology*. New York: Bantam Books, 1972. Includes a highly readable synopsis of Cortes's conquest and does an excellent job of placing it in historical perspective.

Hernando Cortes, *Hernan Cortes: Letters from Mexico*. Translated by A. R. Pagden; introduction by J. H. Elliott. New York: Grossman Publishers, 1971. The letters provide a very detailed account of the conquest. Occasionally, Cortes makes mistakes on his dates.

Bernal Diaz [del Castillo], *The Conquest of New Spain*. Translated by J. M. Cohen. New York: Penguin Classics, 1976. Probably the most dependable source on the conquest, this book is a vigorous account by a soldier who fought in every battle. Diaz describes Cortes at his best and worst.

———, *The Discovery and Conquest of Mexico: 1517–1521*. Translated by A.P. Maudslay. Philadelphia: Farrar, Straus, and Cudahy, 1956. The classic translation of the most important eyewitness account of Cortes's conquest.

Wallace K. Ferguson, *Europe in Transition: 1300–1520*. Boston: Houghton Mifflin, 1962. Overview of events in Europe in the time leading up to Cortes's conquest.

Patricia de Fuentes, trans., *The Conquistadors: First Person Accounts of Mexico*. New York: Orion Press, 1963. Includes two small but critically important accounts of Cortes in Mexico.

Francisco Lopez de Gomara, *Cortes: The Life of the Conqueror*. Translated and edited by Lesley Byrd Simpson. Los Angeles: University of California Press, 1964. Written with Cortes's help and documents, this biography spans the subject's entire life; it is one of the main contemporary sources on the conqueror.

Hubert Herring, *A History of Latin America from the Beginnings to the Present*, 3rd ed. New York: Knopf, 1972. A standard survey of Latin America from the colonial period to the 1970s; includes explanations of Spanish colonial policies.

Paul Horgan, *Conquistadors in North American History*. Greenwich, CT: Fawcett Publications, 1965. One of the most readable accounts of Spain's conquest of the Americas.

Hammond Innes, *The Conquistadors*. New York: Knopf, 1969. Supplies information about the conquest and the political situation that existed in Europe at the time.

William Weber Johnson, *Cortes*. Boston: Little, Brown, 1975. An insightful look into Cortes's life; his recent unpopularity in Mexico is noted especially.

Francis Clement Kelly, *Blood Drenched Altars: Mexican Study and Comment*. Milwaukee: Bruce Publishing, 1935. Written before the current emphasis on multiculturalism, Kelly straightforwardly defends Cortes's actions in Mexico.

Bartolomé de Las Casas, *Tears of the Indians*. Translated by Sir Arthur Helps. Williamstown, MA: John Lilburne Company, 1970. Intended as a general condemnation of Spanish treatment of the Indians, this book was widely distributed throughout Europe in translations. More than any single work it helped create the Black Legend of Spanish cruelty towards natives.

William H. Prescott, *Conquest of Mexico*. New York: Book League of America, 1843, 1934. Prescott, a blind scholar working in the early 1800s, wrote the book by which all accounts of Cortes and the conquest are judged.

Henry Morton Robinson, *Stout Cortez: A Biography of the Spanish Conquest*. New York: Century, 1931. Written long before the influence of multiculturalism, Robinson's account portrays Cortes in heroic terms.

Fray Bernardino de Sahagun, *General History of the Things of New Spain*. Translated by Arthur J. O. Anderson and Charles E. Dibble. Santa Fe, NM: School of American Research, and the University of Utah, Monographs of the School of American Research, 1975. Translated from Aztec texts after the conquest, Sahagun's work provides an Indian view of Cortes.

Anne Terry White and William Brandon, *The American Indian*. New York: Random House, 1963. A very readable survey describing the Indians from Central America to Canada. Beautifully illustrated with paintings and photographs.

Index

Picture Credits

Cover photo by Hulton Deutsch Collection Limited

Courtesy Department Library Services, American Museum of Natural History, 55 (top), 62, 77, 80, 81 (top)

The Bettmann Archive, 25, 34, 55 (bottom), 98

The Bodleian Library, Oxford, 41

Brown Brothers, 10, 23, 32, 42

Culver Pictures, Inc., 29, 33

Giraudon/Art Resource, NY, 40, 71

By permission of the Houghton Library, Harvard University, 17

Hulton Deutsch Collection Limited, 9, 52, 76, 86

The Institute of Texan Cultures, 60

Library of Congress, 11, 15

Mercado/Art Resource, NY, 38, 46, 64

The New York Public Library, Rare Book Division, 27, 100

North Wind Picture Archives, 19, 20, 22, 28, 56, 58 (both), 63, 67, 69, 78, 81 (bottom), 83, 84, 89, 93

Peter Newark's Western Americana, 14, 36, 48, 49, 61, 75, 82

Reuters/Bettmann, 96

Stock Montage, Inc., 26, 35, 39, 44, 45, 51, 72

UPI/Bettmann, 97

About the Author

A native of Elsberry, Missouri, who has taught in public schools for twenty-three years, Stephen Lilley holds a master's degree in history. He also performs as a traditional jazz musician and is a freelance author.